D1293319

ANXIETY
IN
CHRISTIAN EXPERIENCE

Other books by the author

The Christian Pastor

The Bible in Pastoral Care

Where to Go for Help

The Revelation of God in Human Suffering

Religious Factors in Mental Illness

Religious Dimensions of Personality

What Psychology Says About Religion

Christ and Selfhood

Protestant Pastoral Counseling

Pastoral Counseling and Social Problems

Alcohol: In and Out of the Church

The Holy Spirit in Five Worlds

On Becoming Children of God

When Religion Gets Sick

New Dimensions of Pastoral Care

Anxiety
in
Christian Experience

by
WAYNE E. OATES

WORD BOOKS, *Publisher*
Waco, Texas

ISBN 0-87680-204-8

Library of Congress Catalog Card No.: 55-8184

Scripture quotations from the Revised Standard Version of the Bible, copyright 1946 and 1952, by the Division of Christian Education of the National Council of Churches, are used by permission.

First Printing, June 1971
Second Printing, April 1974
Third Printing, July 1976

PRINTED IN THE UNITED STATES OF AMERICA

To

Mr. and Mrs. Charles Edwin Gheens

CONTENTS

PREFACE

Three lines of insight and discipline converge to make the painful uneasiness of mind known as anxiety meaningful both to the participating Christian and to his pastoral counselor: the insights and disciplines of the Biblical message, the findings of modern psychotherapists, and the clinical experience of pastoral counselors. These sources of understanding of the problem of anxiety bear witness together to reinforce each other and separately to throw light upon each other.

This book represents the effort to deal systematically with the problem of anxiety in Christian experience, drawing upon these three converging lines of understanding. Materials are drawn from the Bible, contemporary psychotherapy, and clinical pastoral experience to define, clarify, and illustrate different types of anxiety and their interlocking relationship to each other as anxiety moves from one depth of meaning to another in Christian experience. It needs to be made clear that this is not an attempt to "harmonize" total systems of psychotherapy with the Bible or vice versa. The problem of anxiety is the point of concern in this discussion, and materials from the Bible, psychotherapy, and clinical pastoral experience are chosen in terms of their relevance to this problem and only incidentally in terms of a comparative study of Biblical and psychotherapeutic doctrines, per se.

Anxiety is a reaction of tension to threats to the selfhood of an individual or to the groups to which he belongs and for which he feels responsible. It manifests itself at different levels of meanings in terms of the way it becomes conscious to him in his at-

9

tempts to identify and deal with his painful uneasiness of mind. Different types of anxiety, therefore, are described in the following chapters. These different types of anxiety are related to each other in a blending spectrum of human tensions. They are separated only in the refraction process of analysis and in terms of the particular shading of anxiety which takes predominance in the consciousness of the anxious person. Any one of these types of anxieties is related implicitly, if not explicitly, to all the others, from the "easily talked about" character of economic anxiety to the unutterable depths of holy dread.

The problem of anxiety, as it appears in the spiritual pilgrimage of contemporary men and women, presents a basic issue in any adequate psychology of religious experience. The needs of anxious persons focus the message of Biblical and psychological truth, on the one hand, with the theory and practice of pastoral counseling, on the other hand, in what may be called a "bifocal" view of *what* Christian experience in fact and process really is. The result is a living and moving vision of the drama of redemption in Christ into which God has chosen to encompass the fretful struggles of men. In one particular sense, anxiety and Christian experience are akin: both are vital, alive and never static, and their process is never written on tablets of stone, but always on tablets of human hearts. An ordered description of the process of anxiety in Christian experience, impossible to catch adequately on the printed page, is the hoped for result of these pages.

Such an approach to the psychology of Christian experience, it is hoped, will serve as a theological basis for effective pastoral counseling. This will help to prevent unexamined techniques, devoid of Biblical understanding, from becoming neat tricks for tinkering with people's souls. Such superficial pastoral counseling misses the larger meanings of men's restless anxieties over self-preservation. It fails to grasp the secret of the inner peace of courageously self-dedicated persons in the "fellowship of concern" who, nevertheless, are "genuinely anxious" about the things of the Lord Jesus Christ.

The aim, therefore, of this book is not to provide a group of easy answers to " how to " questions, but to take the reader on a pilgrimage with anxious people as they, in a sense, " descend into hell " and are born, as alive from the dead, to walk in the newness of life in the Kingdom of God.

WAYNE E. OATES

Louisville, Kentucky

ACKNOWLEDGMENTS

The persons who have confided their inmost anxieties to the author in counseling interviews have his reverential regard and continuing gratitude for permitting him to reveal the biographies of their anxieties. The students at the Southern Baptist Theological Seminary and Union Theological Seminary in New York have participated with the author in the refinement of the ideas presented here. Professors G. S. Dobbins, Henlee Barnette, and Wayne E. Ward have read either all or part of the manuscript and given creative suggestions for clarification and expansion of the pattern of thinking in these pages.

The author owes a real debt of gratitude to Mrs. Wallace Denton for typing, proofreading, and making innumerable editorial suggestions for improving this manuscript. With the pressure of her schedule as a teacher in a nursery school, she added this task to her program at great expenditure of devoted effort. Without her patience and precision, this manuscript would have been trebly difficult to complete.

Christmas is at hand as this book is finished. The author is grateful to God that he can spend the Christmas season with his family and " be anxious for nothing " — especially this book!

ECONOMIC ANXIETY

I. The Reality of Economic Anxiety

Recent prosperity has tended to gloss over the fact that poverty can be real. Psychological teachings, in behalf of a deep insight into human self-deceptiveness, have tacitly discounted economic anxieties as being superficial. The child, however, who is told from his earliest memory that he is "just one more mouth to feed" by a father who cannot find work or who drowns his sense of inadequacy as a wage earner in alcohol does not doubt the reality of poverty. The missionary who spent three years in a Japanese concentration camp, knowing hunger acutely enough to think of cannibalism, did not consider the need for food as symbolic of something else, or symptomatic of some deeper need. It was real in itself. The family that lived from day to day during the great depression on berries picked from wild bushes and on bread from the Emergency Relief Administration did not have to beg the children to eat the vegetables that they did not have. Rather, their anxiety threw them into emotional chaos as each morsel of food was snatched at by all.

Anxiety over food and economic security distills and clarifies personality up to a certain point, but beyond that it devastates the whole man. Anxiety over a surplus of wealth can create similar results. In both instances, economic anxiety is real, exerts the "tyranny of the tangible" over other areas of the whole life of the person, and serves as one of the sharpest indicators of trouble in the feelings persons have toward themselves and others.

The breadwinner of a family gets sick. He is hospitalized and his whole economic routine is disrupted. This "very present" concern, apart from the fact that he is sick, is the care of his family. If, because of illness, he becomes partially or permanently disabled, the resulting economic disorganization presents a painful uneasiness of mind. His whole concept of himself as an adequate husband, father, and breadwinner undergoes radical revision.

A seventeen-year-old boy borrows his father's car to take his girl for a ride. They have a wreck that is not covered by insurance. Luckily they are not killed, but the girl has to have expensive plastic surgery on her face. Both cars are demolished and the bills for all these things are the responsibility of the frightfully anxious and panic-stricken boy. He cannot think except in terms of this acute problem and how to solve it. Will his whole sense of destiny and his vocational plans be revised as he meets this particular crisis?

Another person, a veteran in his early twenties, gets mad at his girl friend's sister and slaps her. She calls the police and has him arrested. He works for a company that has an inflexible rule that anyone who is arrested is automatically fired. The young man, the sole support of his widowed mother and his younger sister, loses his job. Great lines of decision are tangled up in this confused situation, but the pressing problem of next week's rent and grocery bill, temporal as they are, crowds out all others in the conscious concerns of the young man.

When the tangible concern of finding bread consumes the waking hours of a person, the more subtle and highly introspective anxieties are seemingly of little importance to him. As one young German student answered when asked whether the field of pastoral counseling had developed in Germany after the war as it had in America: " No," he said, " we have been so involved in the more pressing issues of food and shelter that we have had little time to spend with nameless troubles." A sort of companionship of misery develops among the poverty-stricken and the hunger-ridden in which the niceties of manners, the keeping of social secrets, and the conventions of society mean less to them. For instance, Harold S. Guetzkow and Paul H. Bowman of the University of Minnesota conducted hunger experiments with students who voluntarily submitted themselves to starvation " in the hope that their privation might help millions who starve involuntarily " in war-stricken and famine areas. They discovered that

" One of the most profound changes which took place was the decreased sociability of the men. . . . The men built up a tremendous in-group feeling that tended to exclude both their nonstarving friends and the administrative and technical staff. They were especially alienated by the individual who supposed he knew what it was like to be hungry, because he had gone without food for a couple of days. It was hard to sit next to one's comrade who had extra food. They became provoked at the laboratory staff for giving 'too much' food to some, and thought it criminal to restrict the rations of others, even though they understood that the experimental plan demanded such adjustments in rations." (Guetzkow and Bowman, *Men and Hunger,* p. 30. Brethren Publishing House, 1946.)

The reality of hunger and the pressing anxieties it creates overrule even moral considerations and religious rituals and requirements. For instance, the Pharisees saw the disciples of Jesus plucking ears of grain to eat and criticized them for doing so on the Sabbath. Jesus reminded them of the behavior of David, who, " when he was hungry, and those who were with him: how he entered the house of God and ate the bread of the Presence, which it was not lawful for him to eat nor for those who were with him." Even so, the child of a displaced person's family became delinquent when thrust on the streets to fend for himself, plundering food stores, stealing money, and distrusting mankind in general.

II. The Blinding Power of Economic Anxiety

Economic anxiety is real in many instances and commensurate with the actual situation in which the anxious person is involved. Furthermore, its very reality *blinds* the person to other needs and anxieties that bear in upon his spirit. The glare of this anxious stress distorts a person's perception of his total needs and he loses perspective as he attempts to deal with life as a whole. The conscious life of the individual is inundated with economic anxiety, and all other concerns are submerged by it.

For instance, a psychiatrist referred the young wife of a psychotic man to the author. The couple were hard-pressed economically. The psychiatrist was virtually giving his services to the sick husband, who was a member of the same church to which the psychiatrist himself belonged. The wife needed separate counseling, and the doctor felt that a nonmedical counselor could help her.

However, after she had come for three interviews, the author realized that she could not progress at all in understanding her husband and taking a more mature position in relation to him. Each time she confronted this necessity, her courage failed her because of her anxiety over the rent which was overdue, the bill for the two-year-old daughter's milk which was two months behind, and the fear that fuel for the house was soon to be cut off. The help of a social agency was called in and the budgetary problem was relieved by economic assistance both from the agency and the church under the guidance of a social caseworker. Instruction was given in the ways whereby the whole situation might be placed upon a sounder economic footing. When this was done, the vicious circle of the inability of the couple to mature, in turn, was broken because economic anxiety had been systematically relieved.

This particular couple had married at the very early age of fifteen (for their social group), before they had actually learned to make a living. As is often the case, the economic anxiety generated in an early marriage became the thing upon which all the other problems of the couple were pegged. In anxious attempts to solve these inadequacies, the husband and the wife had both become uncontrollably upset as their basic immaturities were activated.

III. The Typical Complications of Economic Anxiety

Economic anxiety, in addition to being real and blinding, repeatedly complicates other everyday and typical needs of the individual, the family, and the social group. In fact, economic anxiety may hinder insight into other more basic needs of the anxious person. For example, the need for status and place in society, apparent in the struggles of people who have become aware of the social ladder and the need to climb socially, is often complicated by conscious anxiety over salary, business success, etc., in businesses and professions.

Outside the work situation itself, the settled patterns of social class have been disrupted by the improved condition of labor, the rapid accession of wealth by persons not accustomed to having it, and the preoccupation of people generally with the power of various gadgets to symbolize social class status. For instance, newly rich persons often are not sufficiently cultured and educated to participate comfortably with the social class in which their money would otherwise permit them to associate. They find themselves quite isolated and anxious as they seek acceptance in this club, and that order, and reach for other types of social recognition. They may even console themselves with more and more expensive symbols of class, such as gadgets and grown people's toys, i.e., larger automobiles, motorboats, beach houses, etc.

The cleavages of society into in-groups of the ascending and descending gradations of " having " and " not having " represent the ways in which people feverishly set themselves apart from each other in anxious economic competition with each other. Dostoevsky vividly describes the isolation wrought by these complications of the prestige needs of people with anxiety over their economic situations:

" The isolation that prevails everywhere, above all, in our age — it has not fully developed, it has not reached its limit yet. For everyone strives to keep his individuality as apart as possible, wishes to secure the greatest possible fullness of life for himself; but meantime all his efforts result not in attaining fullness of life but self-destruction, for instead of self-realization he ends by arriving at complete solitude. All mankind in our age have split up into units, they all keep apart, each in his own groove; each one holds aloof, hides himself and hides what he has, from the rest, and he ends by being repelled by others and repelling them. He heaps up riches by himself and thinks, ' how strong I am now and how secure,' and in his madness he does not understand that the more he heaps up, the more he sinks into self-destructive impotence. For he is accustomed to rely upon himself alone and to cut himself off from the whole; he has trained himself not to believe in the help of others, in men and in humanity, and only trembles for fear he should lose his money and the privileges that he has won for himself." (Fyodor Dostoevsky, *The Brothers Karamazov,* p. 375, Modern Library, Inc., 1943. Used by permission.)

The futility of such complicated involvements of economic anxiety takes a drastic toll on family life. For instance, the mother of two children whose husband had divorced her was suffering from acute anxiety and confusion of mind. However, the main force of her conscious worries centered upon her loss of status in the community rather than the fact that her husband had left her. She had had to leave the fashionable subdivision of the East End and the Woman's Club of which she was a part and move to the West End in an apartment over her father's grocery store!

Economic anxiety, it is obvious from this last reference, can become complicated with serious marital difficulties which fester at the point of the " money troubles " of the couple and hinder them from communicating realistically with each other. The wife charges that there is not a fair division of the family income, and her husband is said to dole out the money to her. The husband complains that his wife is extravagant and that he cannot trust her with the financial management of the home. The husband may actually be an inadequate wage earner, as is often the case in situations where the couple married and had children very early in life, before they had become competent wage earners. The man's concept of himself is threatened. He may have to depend upon his wife to help earn the living. His anxiety may be doubled by his wife's need to dominate him by continuing to work long after the necessity for her doing so is past.

IV. The Pathological Complications of Economic Anxiety

Economic anxiety, furthermore, may become so deeply complicated with more unconscious distortions in personality as to be a predominant presenting symptom in some pathological conditions of personality. Some interesting research has been done at this point by Edmund Bergler, a psychoanalytically oriented psychiatrist, who has written a book entitled *Money and Emotional Conflicts* (Doubleday & Company, Inc., 1951). He seeks to identify and describe what he calls a " money neurosis." In a discussion of the " psychological problem of money," Bergler rules out the possibility of a separate instinctual drive to possess, and says that what is clinically observable is the way that childish ideas of grandeur and omnipotence with such subtle ease shift themselves to the problem of money. He dubs this process " shifted omnipotence." He says that

"neurotic tendencies come first, and the misuse of money for exactly these, only much later, can be adduced from the shameful, rather barbaric patterns of some neurotic mothers and fathers. Out of quite logical expectations of inheritance they have made a bargaining point for the purpose of imposing their whims and their presence upon their adult children. Through the course of the years I have analyzed many neurotics with the 'inheritance complex.' . . . They had mothers (these were in the majority) who acted as if their sons, daughters, sons- and daughters-in-law had no life of their own but were born for the one purpose: to please them, to cater to them, and to suit them exclusive of all others. The patients' complaints were all similar in context: extraordinary demands for companionship, the parents' presence in their homes, or vice versa, the constant demands for time, the need to adapt to one's taste, and opinions and mode of behavior. Frequently they reported that the big stick (the last will and testament) was shaken in their faces. Said one such victim of his mother's 'emotional dictatorship': 'I have either to postpone my life until my mother dies or renounce my inheritance.'" (Pp. 16, 17, in *Money and Emotional Conflicts,* by Edmund Bergler. Copyright, 1951. Reprinted by permission of the publishers, Doubleday & Company, Inc.)

Bergler incisively compares the healthy and neurotic management of economic anxiety. He schematizes the normal vs. the neurotic relationship to money as follows:

" Normally, money is a means to an end, that end the acquiring of things one desires.

" Neurotically, money is an end per se.

" Normally, one tries to make money as best he can and as much as he can, but in the process will not sacrifice either health, love, hobbies, recreation, or contentment to this end.

" Neurotically, money becomes the center of life; everything else — health, love, hobbies, recreation, and contentment — is subordinated to the urge to possess it.

" Normally, money has no infantile strings attached to it.

" Neurotically, money is a blind for existing and repressed infantile conflicts.

" Normally, the spending of money is taken for granted; it needs no surgical operation to put a dollar into circulation.

" Neurotically, the possession and hoarding of money becomes the predominant motif.

" Normally, unjustified demands for money are warded off (out of necessity) in a matter-of-fact way.

" Neurotically, demands or requests for money generate fury, excitement, and indignation.

" Normally, the phrase ' I cannot afford it ' is a simple statement of an objective fact."

" Neurotically, the phrase, ' I cannot afford it ' represents a defensive triumph against psychic masochism."

(*Ibid.*, pp. 18, 19.)

Another example of the pathological involvements of economic anxiety is to be found in certain cases of the male homosexual. The work and economy of this person quite often is in sad repair. He moves from job to job and from town to town and looks for a male paramour who will relieve him of economic anxiety as a wage earner. He quite often assumes the female social role and stays home, keeps house, dresses lavishly, and cultivates himself aesthetically. One particular man exemplifies this. He grew up as the oldest child with several sisters in a lower-

lower class industrial home. His father was a chronic alcoholic who never provided even the necessities of food for the family. His mother eked out a bare existence for her children and her alcoholic husband.

The boy became fond of fine goods, unusual clothing, and aesthetic luxuries of music and fine books. He said at the age of twenty-two that he considered " work to be vulgar." He was constantly borrowing money, starting charge accounts and leaving them, renting and furnishing apartments for himself and his " boy friends," and pursuing a mythical music and art career against persistent discouragement from people of those professions.

He finally moved to a large city, where his activities were carried on anonymously. It is granted that many psychological roots produce this kind of fruit; nevertheless, economic anxiety seems to be dynamically and symptomatically evident in certain homosexual personalities.

Edmund Bergler further notes what he calls " the inheritance complex." He points out the way in which the child of a wealthy — and sometimes not so wealthy — family may grow up with the time-bound destiny of maintaining the family fortune. He may fashion his every attitude around the hope of being included to the fullest in the inheritance when the parents make their will and die. He may spend his whole life waiting for his parents to die! Naturally, this blinding inhibits his larger realization of an abundant life and the achievement of his own selfhood.

The author has observed this in clinical pastoral practice as it has worked out in the anxieties of parishioners over the family fortune. The mother of one young woman disinherited her daughter from the tiny family inheritance because the daughter married a man who did not belong to her own denomination. She continually wrote her daughter letters of a vindictive nature, telling her that she was praying that her daughter would repent and come back to her mother's faith. The point at which this person came to the author was in the course of a severe depression which called for medical attention in addition to pastoral care. In another case, this same facet of the total life problem of a parishioner appeared when the father of the counselee in question remarried and rewrote his will with his second wife as the chief beneficiary. The counselee, having seen his father bring the prospective second wife to church, left the church and vowed that he would never return again as long as " that woman " sat in his mother's place. For thirteen years he kept this vow of hatred. He began the whole discussion of the matter with the author by saying that the whole situation began when his father forced him to move from the farm that was to be his in the inheritance!

V. The Counsel of Jesus and Economic Anxiety

Jesus himself counseled with persons who brought out their economic anxieties. For instance, one man brought an inheritance complaint to him. The man said, " Teacher, bid my brother divide the inheritance with me." But Jesus said to him, " Man, who made me a judge or divider over you? " Then Jesus told the parable of a man whose land was so prosperous that he did not know what to do with all the goods that it produced. He purposed to tear down his barns and build larger ones, and then he could say to himself, " Soul, you have ample goods laid up for many years; take your ease, eat, drink, be merry." But God said to him: " Fool! This night your soul is required of you; and the things you have prepared, whose will they be? "

This passage comes clear by applying T. W. Manson's principle of interpretation which emphasizes *the audience to whom the words were spoken.* (T. W. Manson, *The Teaching of Jesus: Studies of Its Form and Content,* second edition, pp. 15 ff. Cambridge University Press, 1935.) Jesus was speaking the parable to or concerning a man who was having a quarrel with his brother as to how to divide an inheritance, a treasure that had been laid up. The real judgment fell upon the person who had bequeathed the inheritance, presumably the father of the two brothers. He must have been much like many modern fathers who anxiously labor to build up a fortune, neglecting the emotional security and spiritual development of himself and his sons. He thought that in providing an inheritance for them he was doing them good as well as making a name for himself. But now that his life has been required of him, his own sons are asking the question, " The things you have prepared, whose will they be? "

The sons, on the other hand, had all their lives lived with the inheritance as their chief concern. They had visualized what they would be able to do with " their part." They had not been children of a parent who would divide his living between them as did the father in the story of the Prodigal Son and the Elder Brother. They had put aside all the persuasive appeals of those who would challenge them to " leave the dead to bury their own dead " in order to go and proclaim the Kingdom of God.

These two sons remind one in some respects of the rich young ruler. Jesus' appeal to him to sell all he had and give it to the poor very easily could have been a challenge to unsaddle himself of the inheritance obligations which kept him from ever being anything but an altar boy in his father's shrine of wealth! Haggai describes such a fate in his plaintive insight:

" You have sown much, and harvested little; you eat, . . . but you never have your fill; you clothe yourselves, but no one is warm; and he who earns wages earns wages to put them into a bag with holes " (Hag. 1:6).

Work, economic gain, and accumulated wealth to Jesus were not an all-out effort to be consumed in such a meaningless end.

The sequel to the story of the Rich Young Ruler indicates, nevertheless, that Jesus was aware that not everyone was spiritually prepared to make the leap of faith to a more meaningful existence. He did not attempt to overpersuade the man to make an outward commitment to a program of healing fellowship when essentially his heart was fixed on his inner idolatry of wealth. Jesus saw the need of even his closest disciples for reassurance when he told them, in the light of their participation with him in his adventure of the Kingdom:

"Truly, I say to you, there is no one who has left house or brothers or sisters or mother or father or children or lands, for my sake and for the gospel, who will not receive a hundredfold now in this time, houses and brothers and sisters and mothers and children and lands, with persecutions, and in the age to come eternal life. But many that are first will be last, and the last first." (Mark 10:29-31.)

VI. Certain Theological Issues in Economic Anxiety

From a strictly theological point of view, economic anxiety was linked with sin and guilt in the Old and New Testament thought of God. This is clearly in the thought of the psalmist in Ps. 112:1-3.

> "Praise the Lord.
> Blessed is the man who fears the Lord,
>   who greatly delights in his commandments!
> His descendants will be mighty in the land;
>   the generation of the upright will be blessed.
> Wealth and riches are in his house;
>   and his righteousness endures for ever."

Jesus contradicted this settled assumption in his disciples' minds when he taught them concerning the rich young man:

"And the disciples were amazed at his words. But Jesus said to them again, 'Children, how hard it is to enter the kingdom of God! It is easier for a camel to go through the eye of a needle than for a rich man to enter the kingdom of God.' And they were exceedingly astonished, and said to him, 'Then who can be saved?'" (Mark 10:24-26.)

As Major, Manson, and Wright say concerning this passage:

"His disciples . . . were astonished at this statement. The Jews of this period viewed the possession of wealth as a mark of divine favor. 'The blessing of the Lord maketh rich, and He addeth no sorrow to it,' was a saying of the wise. On the other hand, it was the families of evil men who were supposed to fall into poverty." (H. D. A. Major, T. W. Manson, and C. J. Wright, *The Mission and Message of Jesus,* p. 131. E. P. Dutton & Co., Inc., 1938.)

In the Old Testament, wealth was supposed to be a sure sign of God's approval, and poverty a sure sign of hidden sin. Some of the rabbis of that day had taken the doctrine of God's providential care in the basic necessities and simplicities of life to mean also that if a person would be good according to the law, he would prosper exceedingly. Even today spiritually immature people interpret this to be true. But the great theodicies of Job and Jeremiah bravely include the question, Why do the wicked prosper? The attitude of the proverb of the Old Testament reflects a humorous maturity of judgment:

> "Remove far from me falsehood and lying;
>   give me neither poverty nor riches;
>   feed me with the food that is needful for me,
> lest I be full, and deny thee,
>   and say, 'Who is the Lord?'
> or lest I be poor, and steal,
>   and profane the name of my God."
>   (Prov. 30:8,9.)

In the second place, economic anxiety is obviously related to a "works theology." Men anxiously try by works to *earn* the right to peace with themselves and God by continually *redoubling their efforts*. The rich fool said to himself, after he had redoubled his efforts and built bigger barns in which to trust, "Soul, . . . take your ease." The Children of Israel, when told to gather quail and manna for the needs of the day, redoubled their efforts and sought to lay up more than was necessary in order to be secure. They substituted faith in their own efforts for the faithfulness of God. In doing so, they thought they would release their anxiety and be secure. They sought to lay up treasures of food, but in turn it spoiled and was no good to them. Instead of easing their anxiety, they confounded themselves with futility and meaninglessness. Both the rich fool and the Israelites looked upon their redoubled efforts and their accumulation of things as a way of resolving their uneasiness of mind and achieving inner security.

Jesus cautioned against this fictitious search by saying, "Do not lay up for yourselves treasures on earth, where moth and rust consume and where thieves break in and steal." This is not a condemnation of the wise management of food, clothing, and shelter, whereby the fat years of plenty are used to offset the ravages of the lean years of poverty and famine. The "ever-normal granary" economy was enjoined by Joseph in Egypt. Also, Jesus told the parable of the Foolish Man who set out to build a house without first counting the cost. Rather, these teachings concerning economic anxiety are aimed at the fictitious goal of absolute economic security. The burden of economic anxiety has no permanent temporal solution. It does have a daily solution, as men learn to pray, "Give us this day our daily bread." This was the one prayer for tangible things that Jesus taught. To assume that the amassing of economic resources is the end intention rather than the means of achieving more enduring satisfaction of life is "a guiding fiction" and an evident kind of idolatry in itself. Such an idolatry is man's puny affirmation of his supposed self-sufficiency, his exertion of an imagined omnipotence, and his refusal to accept the burden of anxiety characteristic of his finite nature. Jesus said, "No one can serve two masters."

The redoubling of one's efforts to release economic or any other kind of anxiety is the emotional basis for what might be called a "works" theology, earning security before God. The child who feels rejected by his parents often strains every nerve to do something that will win his parents' favor. The Christian who feverishly attempts "to prove his worth" to God is not unlike this child. And, in retrospect, when he has achieved temporal success he is likely to try to relax his anxious state of mind by telling himself his success is a sign that he is righteous, and giving thanks that he is not like other men. Even his attempts at relaxation become "relax as hard as you can" efforts for a new kind of success without raising any question about his idolatry of the works of his own hands. Faith without works is dead; works without faith is *anxious*. The "god of this world" has blinded his mind to keep him "from seeing the light of the gospel of the glory of Christ, who is the likeness of God."

When the light is clear and the economically anxious person is no longer afraid to look, he sees the cross of Jesus as directly related to the release of his anxiety. When Jesus entered his ministry, he himself endured the anxiety involved in the ability to turn stones into bread when the pangs of physical hunger were upon him. He refused to take the deceptive short cut of economic success, and immediately was strengthened by the Holy Spirit in the clarified relationship of trust and love between him and the Heavenly Father. He had hardly made this dedication, however, before he was thrust into his ministry to the hungry multitudes of Palestine. Great crowds gathered, but they had nothing to eat. Their anxiety was real (Mark 8:1 ff.)! The dedication of Jesus, therefore, called for the "changing of conditions that make difficult the entrance of Christ — by lifting the valleys (the poverty that embitters and gnaws) and lowering the hills (the wealth that leaves men in blind pride), by smoothing the rough road (the desolate hardships that canker the soul)." (*The Interpreter's Bible,* Vol. VII, p. 263. Abingdon Press, 1951.)

Yet, the miracle of bread blinded the disciples to the fact of the cross and he could only say to them: "Do you not yet perceive or understand? Are your hearts hardened? Having eyes do you not see, and having ears do you not hear?" (Mark 8:17,18.) Jesus could see that their anxiety over bread had blinded them to their deepest needs in relationship to him. The Fourth Gospel interprets this in his words: "You seek me, not because you saw signs, but because you ate your fill of the loaves. Do not labor for the food which perishes, but for the food which endures to eternal life." (John 6:26,27.) Further on in the account he appeals for wholehearted commitment to him and the Kingdom of God as a way of release from their anxiety over bread:

"Jesus said to them, 'I am the bread of life; he who comes to me shall not hunger, and he who believes in me shall never thirst'" (John 6:35).

This kind of commitment is the context in which he gave his most specific teaching about the resolution of economic anxiety through spiritual dedication:

"Do not be anxious about your life, what you shall eat or what you shall drink, . . . what you shall put on. . . . But seek first his kingdom and his righteousness, and all these things shall be yours as well." (Matt. 6:25,33.)

This search for the Kingdom of God and his righteousness is not on a treadmill of self-justification through success in temporal achievements. The search leads one on a pilgrimage to the individual's own particular crucifixion and resurrection of which Paul spoke: "I have been crucified with Christ; it is no longer I who live, but Christ who lives in me; and the life I now live in the flesh I live by faith in the Son of God, who loved me and gave himself for me." (Gal. 2:20.)

The symbol of man's redemption in the death of Christ did not by chance *happen* to be that of the broken bread and poured wine in the body and blood of Jesus Christ. Here are symbols both of economic needs for bread and drink and of the spiritual dedication of these needs to God in the death, burial, and resurrection of Christ. Such a dedication draws men together in spiritual communion rather than setting them apart in economic competition. It develops an attitude of sharing rather than of taking from each other. It results in insight as men and God are known of each other in the breaking of bread, and a third Presence is at hand on every road, even as it was at Emmaus, in the earning and spending of money. The only competition is the competition of love, and everybody wins in a contest of love for each other.

Chapter
2

FINITUDE (ESCHATOLOGICAL) ANXIETY

Man fretfully grasps at the uncertain security of the temporal. When man, as in the case of economic anxiety, sets his heart upon the security of the temporal, succeeds in grasping it, and depends upon it for his ultimate satisfaction, this very satisfaction itself turns to ashes. As Omar Khayyám says, it lights "a little hour or two" and is gone. Such dissatisfaction provokes a deeper kind of anxiety over the illusoriness of the fantasy of an endless temporal existence. Every man knows the answer to Jesus' question: "Which of you by being anxious can add one cubit to his span of life?" (Matt. 6:27.) Economic anxiety is the conscious expression of a deeper and more diffuse kind of anxiety over the shortness of life, the set end of man's days. This anxiety is aptly called "finite anxiety."

On the day that the author wrote this, he interviewed a person who gave a remarkably clear description of the fusion of economic anxiety and finitude anxiety. She told of having found a letter that her mother had written to her uncle. It was during the depression, and the widowed mother had written to her brother, saying, "I do not see how on earth the children and I will be able to live." What the adult mother meant was "to make a living," "to make ends meet," "to keep the budget balanced." But this counselee interpreted her mother's words quite differently: she felt that their death was right at hand! So frightened and anxious was she that she could never tell her mother.

I. Finitude Anxiety and the Stages of Life's Way

The normal process of aging itself provides periodic phases of finitude anxiety in individuals and groups as they confront the reality of death in "installments" of this kind of anxiety. The pastor's crisis ministry is replete with examples of the anxious tremors of members of his flock as they move from one of life's crises to another. (A more complete treatment of this is in the author's book *The Christian Pastor,* Chapter I. The Westminster Press, 1951.) From the chuckle of a little boy of four who lies on the floor and kicks his feet as his daddy works, saying, "I don't want to grow up and have to work like you do," to the shudder of a bereaved person as he absorbs the incalculably heavy blow of the news of the sudden death of his child, the pastor is called upon to participate not only in his own finitude anxiety but also in that of his people.

These stages of growth, aging, and the confrontation of death call for decisions in keeping with the finite necessities of that particular stage of development. (See Lewis J. Sherrill, *The Struggle of the Soul.* The Macmillan Company, 1951.) An individual is subtly reminded that he "will not pass this way again." The doors of destiny swing on small hinges and have one-way locks. As Tillich says: "Every decision excludes possibilities and makes our life narrower. Every decision makes us older and more mature. Youth is openness. But every decision closes doors. . . . Life closes doors in every moment." (Paul Tillich, *Shaking the Foundations,* p. 178. Charles Scribner's Sons, 1950.)

The pastor often deals with finitude anxiety in premarital counseling, particularly in dealing with indecision and the fretful anxiety of engaged couples who are constantly breaking and remaking their engagements. This is often more than just the "spats" of lovers, and runs more deeply in that one or the other (or both) of the couple collides with his or her ambivalent feelings about closing the door of decision behind them on such a promise as to involve doing anything "until death does them part." Likewise, childish fantasies of perfection of a human relationship serve as background scenery for this drama.

Furthermore, the pastor regularly encounters more obvious expressions of finitude anxiety in the lives of physically ill patients whom he visits who are suffering their first serious illness, after never having been sick a day in their lives. They have unconsciously, as Freud said, been living under the illusion that death would happen to everyone *except* them. Now the presence of pain thrusts the factuality of their humanity upon them; the rude awakening to their finitude is at hand in the form of an illness. Their anxieties over their economy, their family, and their work all become acute. The shift from a completely active existence to one of helplessness quickens this anxiety. The patient is not unusual who, on his first illness, becomes highly nervous, difficult to manage from a nursing point of view, and extremely apprehensive if surgery is indicated. He may storm around, boss the nurses, and defy his illness by asserting that his doctors are incompetent.

These examples of typical crises, such as premarital anxiety situations and the anxiety connected with physical illness, give some idea of the way in which finitude anxiety becomes apparent in the common ventures of life. However, deeper manifestations of finitude anxiety are more clearly seen in the more complex concerns of neurotic and psychotic persons. Pastors are, or should be, aware of this basic kind of anxiety of the life situation of such acutely disturbed persons particularly.

Neurotic patients present finitude anxiety to their counseling pastor in the form of the fear of death, the fear of insanity, and occasionally the fear of suicide, in particular, as being uppermost in their thinking. These fears may crystallize into compulsive habits of body and mind that seal off the more general fear of accepting the fact that they are getting older, that they are no longer children (particularly adolescents), and that the "shades of the prison house" of mortality are closing in upon them. The neurotic holds back from his acceptance of his mortality. He is overwhelmed by his childish feelings of omnipotence, an inner fantasy of his immortality, and his feeling of prerogative as an exception to the laws of nature. Otto Rank says that " neurosis as a whole is an individual attempt at healing, against the archenemy of mankind, the death fear, which can no longer be cured by the collective method of earlier ages." (Otto Rank, *Will Therapy*, p. 127. Alfred A. Knopf, Inc., 1945.) As Schopenhauer has said, " Death is the price we pay for life." Rank again says, " The neurotic is a man whom extreme anxiety keeps from accepting the payment of death as the price for life, and who accordingly seeks in his own way to buy himself free from his guilt." Jesus would say that such a person is one who refuses to take up his cross with faith in him for the resurrection. " For whoever would save his life will lose it; and whoever loses his life for my sake and the gospel's will save it." In doing so, Jesus would ascribe as being universally true of all men that which Rank discovered to be true of neurotics in particular.

For instance, a psychiatrist referred one of his patients to the author for religious guidance and pastoral counseling. She told him that she needed God, and that only God could give her a sense of " safeness on the inside." She had married when she was a bit less than seventeen years of age. She and her husband had struggled courageously to overcome the handicap of not being able to make a secure living. Nevertheless, he was continually coping with the fact that he could not reach a maximum economic security for the very reason that he had not trained himself in his twenties to do the kinds of work that earned more money.

Now, at the age of thirty-six, his wife was deeply guilt-laden because at the age of twenty-two she had decided that they were too poor ever to have children. In connection with another routine kind of surgery she had had herself sterilized. She was then caught in the irreversibility of her former decision. Her neurotic fears of leaving her house, of dying, etc., had been dealt with carefully by her psychiatrist. The anxieties she presented to me were not existential in nature, to use Tillich's category for finitude anxiety. She felt herself the victim of fate, meaninglessness, and emptiness. She asked the author if she would ever be free of tension. He frankly told her that she would not, and began to work through with her to the sources of courage whereby she might take the tension upon herself. This was a jolt to her, as she later told her psychiatrist, but it brought her into the prelude of a vital religious reawakening (which is described in the next chapter).

Another example of finitude anxiety appeared in the realm of marriage counseling with a young couple who were handling their fair share of frustrations common to marriage itself with a growing neuroticism, i.e., retreating into minor illnesses, projecting blame upon their poor backgrounds, relating to each other as mother and son, and father and daughter, instead of as man and wife, etc. The counselor did not accept his role as a pastor in such a way as to create the illusion of removing the tensions of adjustment — i.e., the finitude anxiety — concomitant with the basic processes of earning a living, giving and taking hostility, and working out a considerate and understood life routine as man and wife in the first year of marriage. Rather he provided a realistic relationship of understanding in which these could be evaluated for what they were and accepted as such. With remarkable growth and deepened insight, the couple began to communicate more adequately and to accept the responsibility of their new relationship to each other and to the world. At the conclusion of the interview, the husband said a very interesting thing in the light of his study of finitude anxiety. He said, " I am very grateful to you that you did not try to cure us of being human beings! " In turn, the counselor said: " The only way I could have tried that would have been already to have refused to accept my own humanity. To do that would have been to have usurped already the prerogatives of God in your life, and to have attempted to change the way he has made you! "

Finitude anxiety shows up in bold relief in the reaction patterns of particularly disturbed psychotic patients. Occasionally the parish minister meets a psychotic person who presents unusually bizarre religious ideas. The mental hospital chaplain naturally confronts such persons regularly in his work. The following excerpt from a case record of a chaplain's interview of a thirty-one-year-old psychotic man in a mental hospital where he was a patient illustrates this idea. He says:

" I existed before God existed and knew Adam and Eve when they were in the Garden. God said he was going to make man, and I knew it would get him into a lot of trouble, but I didn't try to stop him, because it was his business. As long as I can resist the atoms that come swirling like a black cloud from the planets the world will not come to an end. This is the twentieth century and time is running short."

An apprehension which engulfs the total personality threatens such a patient's existence. Life becomes a mortal conflict between feelings of personal annihilation and a sense of urgency to save the whole world from its own imminent catastrophe and world destruction. Quite often this sense of urgency may systematize itself into a delusional pattern of messianic distortion of the patient's concept of himself. If so, he may present himself as actually being the Christ, or some other exalted personage. Boisen's interpretation of these experiences is that they are essentially problem-solving experiences, in which the individual has come to his extremities without the resources of an accessible community of people with whom he can communicate his unspeakable worries. The psychosis is a drastic attempt to solve the anxiety of finitude, made real in specific problem areas such as marriage, vocation, and self-reference.

The condition of such persons is one of despair as a matter of life and death. It is the result of the persons' having willed to become infinite, and their incapacity to tolerate their own finitude. As Kierkegaard says, " Infinitude's despair is therefore fantastical and limitless." (Sören Kierkegaard, *The Sickness Unto Death,* p. 24. Princeton University Press, 1941.) As Kierkegaard would also say, such persons are lost in possibility for having renounced the limitations of necessity.

II. Patterns of Psychotherapeutic Interpretation of Finitude Anxiety

Modern psychotherapists are asking significant, interpretive questions which help to make finitude anxiety meaningful. This meaningfulness is necessary if anxiety of any kind at any stage is to be bearable. Gotthard Booth, a psychiatrist associated with Columbia University, asks the question:

" Should we expect a 'good society' in which no one will die, a world in which everyone will live eternally, surrounded by successive generations of immortal children? Anyone visualizing this utopia will feel the practical and even the spiritual absurdity of it." (Gotthard Booth, " Health from the Standpoint of the Physician," in *The Church and Mental Health,* edited by Paul Maves, p. 10. Charles Scribner's Sons, 1953.)

He continues by pointing out the unrealistic attitude toward death that much of the propaganda concerning health and medical advance leaves in the minds of people. It overlooks the fact that all people sooner or later die. The same could be said of much of the unrealistic religious teaching concerning death which refers to it as an " error " that needs correcting, an illegitimate intrusion into life, and a fallacious distortion of life itself.

Nicolas Berdyaev detects the weaknesses of such unrealism in his remark that

" Meaning is never revealed in endless time; it is found in eternity. But there is an abyss between life in time and life in eternity, and it can only be bridged by death and the horror of final severance. When the world is apprehended as self-sufficient, completed and closed in, everything in it appears meaningless because everything is transitory and corruptible — i.e., death and mortality in this world is just what makes it meaningless. . . . *The meaning of death is that there can be no eternity in time and that an endless temporal series would be meaningless."* (Nicolas Berdyaev, *The Destiny of Man,* pp. 318, 319. The Centenary Press, 1937.)

Such meaninglessness is implicit in man's attempt to avoid the burden of the anxiety of his finitude, according to Paul Tillich, the theologian who has made use of psychotherapeutic insights. He interprets the experience of Jesus in the wilderness of decision and temptation by saying that Jesus conquered " the forces which tried to make him claim ultimacy for his finite nature. . . . The claim of anything finite to be final in its own right is demonic." (Paul Tillich, *Systematic Theology,* Vol. I, pp. 133, 134. University of Chicago Press, 1951.) In another place in the same volume, Tillich says that " anxiety about transitoriness, about being delivered to the negative side of temporality, is rooted in the structure of being." (*Ibid.,* p. 194.) " To be finite is to be insecure." (*Ibid.,* p. 195.)

Otto Rank, one of the original group of psychotherapists who worked with Freud, sought to add to the meaning of the process of treatment by mobilizing the patient's anxiety over time to the advantage of the recovery of the patient from his neurotic situation. He challenged the method of *endless* analytical sessions which characterized the orthodox techniques of Freud. He saw the process of therapy as being like unto a birth process, with a natural timing " built in," as it were. His aim in therapy " was to shorten analysis. . . . This he did by *setting a definite time* for ending the analysis very early in the course of treatment. When he did this, he states, he found that the patients began to have birth dreams. The thought of leaving the analyst, he believed, brought out all the anxieties of birth." (Clara Thompson, *Psychoanalysis: Evolution and Development,* p. 175. Hermitage House, Inc., 1951.)

The main criticism that Rank leveled at his teacher, Freud, was that the typical Freudian technique of therapy did not come to grips with the reality of time and its relationship to emotional health and growth. The " setting of an end " does just this, and has as its objective, not " completing the therapeutic experience, but of furthering and intensifying it." (Otto Rank, *Will Therapy,* p. 191.) Rank's spontaneous definition of *end setting,* as he names this process, is a " ' last hour ' prolonged." He says that " this ' last hour ' contains a deeper meaning, as the patient actually reacts in case of an ending not prepared for, as if his last hour has come." (*Ibid.*, p. 193.) This kind of treatment is fraught with possibilities for both good and ill, but the main reason for presenting the concept here is that Rank actually sought to bring finitude anxiety "to the head," so to speak, and to mobilize it toward the healing of the patient.

The pastoral counselor is in an excellent position to lay hold of the advantages of Rank's method of end setting. The hard reality of his situation is that his counseling time is necessarily limited. He can say in his own mind and be accurate to the facts that he has only a certain number of interviews which he can give to a particular individual. Then, he has the additional advantage of other professional people upon whom to call when a particular situation calls for more time than he can give to one person. The more arbitrary and mechanical he is about this the more likely he will be to do harm rather than good to the person. However, a careful understanding of the limits of time is one part of the pastor's honest revelation of his limitations to his counselee, his affirmation of his own finiteness, and his refusal to "play god" to the counselee. If he cannot do this, his own finite anxiety may overwhelm him. He overstates himself to the person, permits him to use and exploit him, and finally the counselee exhausts the pastor's patience! However, the quieter and more secure the pastor's realism is at the point of his adjustment to time limits the more apparent will be his own emotional health in the management of his own finitude anxiety.

Another psychotherapeutic insight which is relevant to this discussion of finitude anxiety is Alfred Adler's concept of the inferiority complex. Briefly stated, this theory is that imbalances occur when organic and other types of deviations from the average occur in the total make-up of an individual. A given inferiority may become the nucleus for neurosis through the process of "physical compensation." The neurosis then is the symptom formation of compensatory behavior. Adler says that "the feeling of inferiority, inadequacy, insecurity . . . determines the goal of an individual's existence." (Alfred Adler, *Understanding Human Nature,* p. 72, Greenberg, Publisher, Inc., 1927.) Deep inferiorities — i.e., limitations, weaknesses — stimulate strivings toward superiority. The stronger the inferiority and the deeper the dissatisfaction with the limitations it thrusts upon one, the more fictitious one's goals tend to become. One may "infinitize," as Kierkegaard calls it, i.e., be so overcome by the imagination that one is without limitations or finitude as to be quite convinced of his own omniscience, omnipotence, and godlikeness. As Nietzsche's monster said: "On earth there is nothing greater than I: It is I who am the regulating finger, God." (Friedrich Nietzsche, *Thus Spake Zarathustra,* p. 47, Tudor Publishing Company, 1934.) This, then, is the struggle with the need to be God. Anxiety over one's finitude is a sure evidence of what Kierkegaard called the "eternal qualitative distinction between God and man." To accept this finitude, that man is a mortal and not a god, is the groundwork of redemption. To reject it is the groundwork of guilt and neurosis in which this universally human anxiety begins to crystallize into a nameless guilt which forms all manner of symptoms.

The wag who invented the stock psychiatric joke about the man who had an inferiority complex had more wisdom than he knew when he quoted the psychiatrist as saying to his patient: "You don't have a complex. You really *are* inferior!" The beginning of growth is when a person accepts his limitations, and realizes that he is acceptable in spite of his inferiorities. These inferiorities then become his bond of unity with the rest of humankind, not badges of his isolation from others. They become, not blind driving forces that compel him unconsciously to present a superiority façade that accentuates other people's difference from and inferiority to him. Rather, his inferiorities become marks of the dying of an old self and the birth of a new life of inner security. These inferiorities are no longer the tortuous treadmill of one feverish act of meritorious appeal for approval after another until one faints from exhaustion. These marks of inferiority become transformed into altars of acceptance by *grace,* unearned, unmerited, unsought for — gifts of the Spirit of God.

III. BIBLICAL INSIGHTS INTO THE MEANING OF FINITUDE ANXIETY

The struggle of the soul, just described, leads naturally to a discussion of the Biblical bases for understanding the meaning of this kind of anxiety. A meaningful example of this struggle is set forth in the apostle Paul's biographical account of his severe conflict over his thorn in the flesh. (See II Cor. 12:1-10.) Paul described himself as fluctuating between a need to boast concerning his unusual religious experience and his need to glory in his weaknesses and the power of God to perfect his strength in his infirmities. He interpreted his thorn in the flesh as the epitome of his inferiority and as a constant message from Satan. He begged for its removal until its meaning changed and in doing so changed him. Now it was no longer a "blot on his scutcheon," a symbol of inferiority, but a means of grace whereby the power of God was glorified. This happened through his acceptance of his infirmity, whatever it was, not as a message from Satan reminding him of his inferiority, but as a witness to the finitude that was his. In taking the burden of this anxiety upon himself, he affirmed his humanity. In another connection he said something that accents the reality which he encountered in this divine-human struggle: "But we have this treasure in earthen vessels, to show that the transcendent power belongs to God and not to us" (II Cor. 4:7).

As one turns to the teachings of Jesus concerning finitude anxiety, he sees that Jesus spoke succinctly about the relationship between anxiety on the one hand and the shortness of life when he asked, "Which of you by being anxious can add one cubit to his span of life?" (Matt. 6:27.) Having been bred upon Jewish thought, Jesus was aware of the teachings of the Old Testament which underline again and again the brevity of life and the certainty of its end. This texture of finitude anxiety, as it is woven into the thought of Biblical writers, yields itself plainly in Ps. 39:4-6.

"Lord, let me know my end,
and what is the measure of my days;

let me know how fleeting my life is!
Behold, thou hast made my days a few handbreadths,
     and my lifetime is as nothing in *thy* sight.
Surely every man stands as a mere breath!
Surely man goes about as a shadow!
Surely for nought are they in turmoil;
     man heaps up, and knows not who will gather!"

The psalms refer again and again to the difference between God and man, in that God "knows our frame; . . . that we are dust," that our "days are like grass; like a flower of the field; . . . for the wind passes over it, and it is gone, and its place knows it no more." (Ps. 103:14–16.) "So," the devout Jew prayed, "teach us to number our days that we may get a heart of wisdom." (Ps. 90:12.) These same insights are repeated and set in the Christian context in I Peter 1:24. The practical realism of James 4:13–15 accents the different ways early Christians managed their anxiety over their finitude, as well as the fact of finitude anxiety itself:

"Come now, you who say, 'Today or tomorrow we will go into such and such a town and spend a year there and trade and get gain'; whereas you do not know about tomorrow. What is your life? For you are a mist that appears for a little time and then vanishes. Instead you ought to say, 'If the Lord wills, we shall live and we shall do this or that.'"

Finitude anxiety, as has been repeatedly said, is concerned about the *end* of life, the threats to one's total existence. The Biblical treatment of the problem deals with this kind of anxiety both in terms of the personal existence of the individual and in terms of the cosmic significance of the problem for our interpretation of the history of mankind. As such, one may be faithful to the total message of the New Testament to call this kind of anxiety "eschatological anxiety." Whereas much has been written on the subject of eschatology, the specific correlation of the problems of eschatology with the psychological problems of anxiety, per se, has not been exhaustively studied. This would call for an extensive treatment of both Biblical and clinical data.

However, Amos N. Wilder says that a significant and authoritative examination of the relations of psychology to the whole complex of eschatological conceptions has been made by Anton Boisen in *The Exploration of the Inner World* (Harper & Brothers, 1952). (Amos N. Wilder, *Eschatology and Ethics in the Teaching of Jesus,* revised edition, p. 50. Harper & Brothers, 1950.)

The nature of finitude anxiety in the New Testament is revealed in the encounters of Jesus with the set end to his own earthly pilgrimage in his death on the cross. However, a word of clarification is necessary at this point. The devout Christian often likes to think of Jesus as being devoid of the experience of anxiety. This is rooted in the fallacious conception of anxiety as being *necessarily* bad, or at least something kept out of recognition. Such a view considers anxiety as incidental to man's existence and not basic to it, as peripheral to his purpose in life and not as a part of it, as, in other words, abnormal in every instance and never creatively normal. Such is the subtle implication of teachings like those found in the contemporary " peace of mind " and " positive thinking " literature of Norman Vincent Peale, Joshua Loth Liebman, and Fulton J. Sheen, as well as in superficial interpretations of conversion.

From this perspective, the courage of the Lord Jesus Christ as he faced his own set end of life on the cross, a threat to his total being, gives the problem of " eschatological anxiety " meaning and purpose in the pilgrimage of human life. Jesus bore this kind of anxiety from season to season in his unusually brief life span. He experienced the finitude of his incarnation in the shocks of limitation, mortality, temptation, and hunger in the wilderness decisions. He struggled there with the opportunity to negate his humanity, but chose to accept and affirm the mind and purpose of the Father in sending him. To have done less would have been to have participated in league with the demonic personified.

This anxiety never left Jesus; it only let up for a season. He was acutely aware of " his hour." This is a persistent theme in the Fourth Gospel. The story of the wedding at Cana is marked by the comment of Jesus to his mother: " O woman, what have you to do with me? My hour has not yet come" (John 2:4). He felt the realization of his mission upon him when he said to the woman at the well, "The hour is coming, and now is, when the true worshipers will worship the Father in spirit and truth, for such the Father seeks to worship him" (ch. 4:23). The Johannine Evangelist interprets Jesus' personal safety at two given times as being because "his hour had not yet come" (chs. 7:30; 8:20). In connection with the request of the Greeks to see him and in the prelude to the high-priestly prayer of Jesus (chs. 12:23 and 17: 1, respectively) the thought is expressed: "The hour has come for the Son of man to be glorified." In the first context, the reference is interpreted concerning "what death he was to die" (ch. 12:33). The refining effect of the acceptance of the anxiety concomitant with death on the cross is evident also in the words: "Now is my soul troubled. And what shall I say, 'Father, save me from this hour'? No, for this purpose I have come to this hour. Father, glorify thy name."

(The word for "troubled" in the original text is drawn from a word picture of the Greek which also means "stirring up a crowd." Literally, Jesus was in a tumultuous disturbance within as he came to this hour of decision.)

The eschatological teachings of Jesus, therefore, spring from a deep sense of the impending tragedy of his own existence as well as the affirmation of the finitude, the irreversibility, the limitations, and the "ontological shocks" which normally characterize mankind in the world of time. Jesus, in the eschatological section of Luke's Gospel, associated the anxieties of finite existence with the impending judgment of the inevitable end about to befall the whole earth. The word for "cares" in the following passage is drawn from the same Greek word as a noun as are the words "be anxious" in Matt. 6:27, appearing in the verb form. In fact, an alternate translation is "anxiety":

"But take heed to yourselves lest your hearts be weighed down with dissipation and drunkenness and cares of this life, and that day come upon you suddenly like a snare; for it will come upon all who dwell upon the face of the whole earth. But watch at all times, praying that you may have strength to escape all these things that will take place, and to stand before the Son of man." (Luke 21:34–36.)

IV. CROSS-BEARING AND THE RESOLUTION OF FINITUDE ANXIETY

Paul Tillich, in his book *The Courage to Be* (Yale University Press, 1953), speaks of certain types of "basic anxiety," arising out of man's finitude itself. This anxiety discussed here is basic to man's creaturely nature. The "courage to be" is the willingness to take this anxiety upon oneself and affirm life in the face of it. In short, it means to take up one's cross! In this act is the anxiety of finitude released toward a creative end in God's plan of redemption.

Otto Rank, as has been seen, refers to the need for a collective method of therapy, or plan of redemption. This is the experience of rebirth that comes when man has accepted the reality of death, the fact of his finitude, the weakness of his limitations. Paul talks about the old man or self and the new self. He talks about having been crucified with Christ, having accepted the penalty of death. On the other hand, he speaks of having lived, nevertheless, of having been raised to walk in the newness of life, and of having been released from the bondage of fear unto death. This points toward the possibility of spiritual rebirth upon the acceptance of the fact that by being anxious one cannot add one cubit unto his stature or his span of life. But this life is lived by faith, as Paul describes it:

"Therefore, since we are justified by faith, we have peace with God through our Lord Jesus Christ. Through him we have obtained access to this grace in which we stand, and we rejoice in our hope of sharing the glory of God. More than that, we rejoice in our sufferings, knowing that suffering produces endurance, and endurance produces character, and character produces hope, and hope does not disappoint us, because God's love has been poured into our hearts through the Holy Spirit which has been given to us." (Rom. 5:1–5.)

Such an extraordinary renascence of the spiritual life calls for man's acceptance of the extremities of his existence. When men come to a "dead" end in their pilgrimage, the only choice is to go deeper or higher. This calls for something more than self-gratification: it calls for self-crucifixion of an affirmed finitude anxiety through which men enter into the *nevertheless realm* of true being. Berdyaev is right when he says:

" Death is a manifestation of life, it is found on this side and is life's reaction to its own demand for an end in time. Death cannot be understood merely as the last moment of life followed either by non-being or by existence in the world beyond. Death is an event embracing the whole of life. Our existence is full of death and dying. Life is perpetual dying, experiencing the end in everything, a continual judgment passed by eternity upon time." (*Op. cit.*, p. 319.)

Both psychotherapists and pastoral counselors may unintentionally create the illusion of a life of unlimited satisfaction, divested of the real elements of tension and demand which characterize life itself. On the other hand, the anxiety of finitude can be so completely affirmed as to be the fate of necessity itself without hope in the world. Both instances, enlightened hedonism and defensive stoicism, eliminate the reality of faith and joy in the taking up of one's cross, as it was said of Jesus: " who for the joy that was set before him endured the cross." In the instance of economic anxiety, the power of the anxiety of finitude is turned to man's redemption in the cross. Yet, this direction itself brings to the fore a much more serious and specific kind of anxiety than that which man experiences over his creatureliness, namely, the anxiety of grief and guilt.

THE ANXIETY OF GRIEF

I. GRIEF IN THE PRESENCE OF DEATH

The young man had been married only a short time when it was discovered that his wife had cancer. The disease was diagnosed and an operation was indicated. The doctor informed them that the young bride could live only six months at most. After the operation he reduced his estimate to three months. The husband prayed to God to spare his wife for a year, promising that if he would do so, he, the husband, would do anything for God. His wife lived just short of eleven months and died. The husband felt that his prayer had been answered and outwardly accepted the death with great calmness. He went about his affairs *as if nothing had happened, and the whole community marveled at how he could take it.*

It was not until two years later that any disturbance showed. At that time the young man said that he became cold and indifferent to God, lost fellowship with God, and yet he yearned for the closeness he felt during the weeks following the death of his wife. In the meantime he had remarried, but he and his second wife repeatedly placed flowers in the church on Sunday as a memorial to his first wife. The flood of grief broke through its icy barriers one evening when he came to his pastor's home and sat for two hours pouring out his story of the feelings that had been buried. The spirit of his former wife no longer held him now, although he could never forget the real affection he had

had for her. She was no longer a shrine of the dead before which he worshiped.

The anxiety of grief is the anxiety over a significant loss, or apprehensiveness over the threat of such a loss. The amount of anxiety determines any efforts to comfort the grief-stricken person. Many influences play upon an individual group to produce this anxiety of grief. Notable among these are three particular influences. The depth and quality of relationship between the bereaved person and the person whom he has lost or is about to lose determines the strength of the anxiety of grief. The manner of the death of the loved one also affects the strength of the grief reaction. Death comes as an intruder in many instances, such as sudden deaths from heart attacks, accidents, etc.; violent deaths such as suicide, murder, electrocution; mysterious deaths in which the causes are unknown; and ignoble deaths in which hideous shame attends the grief. On the other hand, death may come as a welcome visitor to very old persons. These different manners of meeting death on the part of the deceased shape the form and intensity of the grief reactions of loved ones. Also, in the third place, the length of the illness of a person before death has a way of making a difference by producing anxiety in "installments of grief" at each new turning of the illness. For instance, the husband of a leukemia patient, whose death came gradually over a period of eight months, said that each time he took her to the hospital hastened and deepened his grief.

II. Grief in the Face of Life

The understanding of grief which restricts itself only to situations in which the anxiety of grief is provoked by the death of a loved one is an incomplete and superficial understanding, however. Life has much more painful and difficult-to-bear losses than those by death. Several examples can be cited, and in these examples the anxiety of grief plays a determinative role.

Mental illness, thanks to advances in psychiatry, is becoming more and more an illness from which people do recover and find

their way through their trouble to a meaningful and useful relationship to their loved ones. However, as a pastor, the author has
moved with families through the deep grief as they have faced
up to the stunning realization that the wife and mother, the
husband and father, the sister or brother would in all probability
never be able to function safely outside a mental hospital. Grief
by death cuts with a sharp edge like unto a razor; grief like this
cuts with the jaggedness of a saw. This problem is not so easily
talked about, and the grief-stricken person suffers much more
isolation and has access to fewer sources of emotional support
than would be true if the loved one had been estranged by death.
Correspondingly, the family's sense of guilt over their real or
imagined part in causing the illness is a predominant source of
anxiety here.

Likewise, pastors and chaplains move through a very real
grief experience with amputation patients to whom they minister. The loss of limb is akin to the loss of life, and the processes
of grief are alike. The amputation patient has many complicating
factors not only in that he suffers anxiety over his loss, but his
infirmity actually militates against his establishing new sources
of interpersonal satisfaction with other people in that he may
feel himself " rejected in advance " because of his handicap. For
instance, a fifty-year-old man lost his wife and two years later
lost his right leg through an accident. His need for companionship from persons of the opposite sex was thwarted by his feeling that his stump was aesthetically offensive to anyone he would
want to go out with. When he went for a conversation with his
pastor he complained that he could neither pray as he ought
to pray nor feel at home in the church. In other words, he expressed his anxiety in terms of estrangement and separation
feelings, typical of the grief reaction.

Another example of the grief reaction is the problem which
appears in the pastoral ministry to persons who have permanently impaired health. A bakery salesman worked two shifts
a day six days a week for four years during the war. He contracted tuberculosis and now his grief is acute over his loss of

health; he condemns himself for the loss of his better body. The anxiety of grief and the anxiety of guilt, as is so often the case, are inseparably intermingled here.

To a lesser degree in broken courtship situations which come to his attention, the pastor counsels with persons suffering from the compounded anxieties of grief and guilt. The anxiety of guilt is in reverse in these two grief situations as compared with situations where the loss of the loved one was by death. In the death of the loved one, the grief experience mobilizes the anxiety of the individual to repress *hostility* which may have been felt toward the deceased. It returns as guilt. However, conversely, the grief of the rejected lover or the divorcee mobilizes the anxiety in the individual to repress the positive feelings of *affection* and *tenderness* toward the estranged mate. These may return in the form of unreasonable depressions and nameless dreads. Divorcees, for instance, have often said during a counseling interview, " I could have accepted all this more easily if he [or she] had died."

Another kind of grief appears behind the façades of religious groups, denominational and interdenominational politics, and even among ministers who are renowned as counselors. Pastors themselves counsel with religious, civic, and political leaders who have been ostracized for one reason or another by those whose approval they considered most worth-while. Pastors encounter this kind of grief in leaders who become scapegoats in order that the community might be cleansed without losing face, atone for its guilt without confessing its sins, and preserve the *status quo* by sacrificing an individual. Such persons, sometimes fellow pastors of pastoral counselors, come for help after having been the scrub board for the dirty linen of a whole tribe. Their entire life purpose has been thwarted by the callousness, inflexibility, and ingrained arrogance of people who are lovers of things as they are. The tragedy of the grief of these persons lies in their isolation. The persons to whom they can turn for guidance and fortification are very few, if not nonexistent. They bear their burdens alone. This is their grief. They are not without guilt themselves, but the treatment given them by their community rarely does much else than confirm them in their needs for self-justification.

One such man turned to the eccentric shoeshop operator in his community for pastoral care after he had been discharged from his job. The quaint old man comforted him in a strange and poignant manner. He said: " They tell me you've been fired from your job. Lot of people feel sorry for you. I don't. I think you have got just what the Lord Jesus said you would get. For years you have been going around here teaching his true gospel as clear as any man among us. He told you they would cast you out for doing so, and that you should rejoice. So don't come in here expecting me to feel sorry for you. If you want me to rejoice with you, I'll be glad to do that."

III. The Process of Grief

The Christian experience of grief is grounded in a spiritual process through which the grief-stricken person lives. The anxiety of grief takes different forms at the successive stages of the grief process. The mourner is comforted best who has some idea of the way in which grief works. The pastor is least nonplused by grief who knows the stages through which his bereaved go as they handle the reaction to deeply significant losses.

The psychotherapists have been especially helpful in the general study of human experience as process of grief. This is particularly true of the experience of grief also. The process of grief has been empirically analyzed in the research of men like Sigmund Freud, Erich Lindemann, Willard Waller, and others. (Sigmund Freud, " Mourning and Melancholia," 1917, *Collected Papers,* Vol. IV, pp. 152–172; Erich Lindemann, " Symptomatology and Management of Acute Grief," *American Journal of Psychiatry,* 101:141–148, 1944; Willard Waller, *The Family: A Dynamic Interpretation,* revised by Reuben Hill. Dryden Press, 1951, Ch. 22, pp. 470–490.) The process through which a grief-stricken person moves has, roughly speaking, about six psychological phases that are fairly easily identified, but which may or may not be telescoped into each other:

1. *The shocking blow of the loss-in-itself.* Shock is an experience elemental to and more primary than most other emotional qualities. Shock is the ruthless thrust of the objective world into the subjective realm of a person's *privatus intellectus* without regard to the absorbing power of that intellect. Shock, therefore, amounts to being hit, struck with a blow, assaulted by reality. The person's anxiety at this stage has not yet been activated, and the momentum of life *as it was* carries him along quite automatically. He acts mechanically and without appropriateness to the real fact of the blow he has received. On one occasion, the author was called to a home to minister to a family whose father-husband had been killed in an industrial accident. The mother was "hit" by the news and fainted. She came back to consciousness and asked what had happened. She was told again of the death, and fainted again. This was repeated five times before she could absorb the blow with full retention of consciousness. As she regained consciousness one time, she asked the author, "Why does God let this have to be so?"

2. *The numbing effect of the shock.* The most characteristic experience of grief-stricken persons, following the shock of the blow, is the numbing effect. This has physiological counterparts similar to the "freezing" power of a local anesthetic. Persons at this time tend to complain that "they can't feel," that "it seems as if they are frozen up inside," and that "their spirits are paralyzed." This seems to be nature taking care of the individual by anesthetizing them emotionally. The feelingful reality of the blow will become broken to them gradually. One of the common spiritual complaints at this stage is that the person cannot feel that God is near. One acutely bereaved person came to her pastor asking him: "How do you think I should feel at this time? I am trying to act like a Christian, but I don't know how to feel any more." His response was: "You seem to feel numb, even in your emotions toward God, and you come to me to find not only a guide for your feelings but also to find the friendship of someone who is in touch with God. Whatever feeling

this numbness gives way to, you may be sure God will accept and understand as you express it to him."

3. *The struggle between fantasy and reality.* Grief is like unto an amputation, when a part of oneself has been cut off. For a time, the organism goes on acting *as if* the lost member is still there. The grief-stricken person struggles over accepting the reality of the loss. The whole inner selfhood of the individual tends to prefer fantasy to the reality. An inner wall of fantasy is built against the reality, and the individual's anxiety takes the form of " steeling oneself " against the break-through of reality upon the cherished fantasies of the departed love object. For instance, two little boys, one seven and the other nine, were scuffling on the floor with their father about a month after their mother had died. One of the boys was being hurt a bit in the scramble, and he cried out, " Mommy, Mommy, make Daddy quit! " Then, with a sudden silence the friendly fight ended, because all of them knew that the mother was no longer there.

4. *The break-through of a flood of grief.* When the wall of fantasy is broken, the grief of the individual floods over him. As the psalmist puts it, " the torrents of perdition assailed me; the cords of Sheol entangled me, the snares of death confronted me " (Ps. 18:4,5). From a psychological point of view, this is a catharsis of the wound of grief. In the loss of someone by death, the explainable symptoms of depression, deep discrepancy feelings, and the draining of life of meaning are obvious. If the grief has been set into action by an interpersonal conflict, the pain is all the more agonizing in that the former friend, now the bereaved person's enemy, can no longer be acknowledged consciously as one whom he or she has ever loved. This is particularly evident in the case of grief after a divorce has been effected.

For instance, deep roots of bitterness sprang up in the life of a woman whose husband had divorced her. She said that she used to pray to God, but now she felt that even God had forsaken her in her loneliness. In the process of counseling with her, her pastor heard her pour out her hostility toward her husband and saw these feelings gradually change into a deep admission of her former love for him and the ways in which she still missed him. This is one dynamic factor that validates a pastor's suggesting a time of separation before a divorce is effected: the normal processes of grief have an opportunity to take place and may effect a deeper kind of insight on the part of both parties. This may occasionally result in a spontaneous reconciliation. Furthermore, a separation may be a kind of insurance that the repressed, unaccepted love energies will not quickly, unconsciously, and blindly attach themselves to some other spouse who is much like the divorced mate.

5. *Selective memory and stabbing pain.* After the catharsis of several waves of severe grief, the process levels off to a more drawn-out and less intense experience of day-by-day reassociation of the memories of the most loved person or object with the fact of the loss. Each time a new reassociation is made, a thrust of grief stabs the individual. He may be walking down the street and see someone who reminds him of the person for whom he is grieving. The pleasantness of the remembrance of the loved one is rudely interrupted with the reality: " She is gone! " " She is dead! " This is followed by stabbing pain and reassociation. Daytime reverie and fantasy may be the way of assuaging this anxiety, and the grief work continues at night in bereavement dreams. These dreams are ridden with anxiety, involving erotic and hostile material which is seeking recognition and reintegration in the consciousness of the person.

The anxiety of grief becomes associated with the anxiety of guilt in that the recriminatory feelings of the individual begin to surface in this and other phases of grief. The hostilities and affections he feels toward the loved one curl back upon him in the form of guilt. Or, in his desperation, he may thrust them forth upon a cosmic scheme and blame God for his plight, asking why God would let such a thing happen if indeed he is God.

6. *The acceptance of loss and the reaffirmation of life itself.* From a psychological point of view, the individual himself undergoes a death, burial, and resurrection of his selfhood in the process of grief, first rejecting life in the face of death and then ac-

cepting death in the face of life. In the losing of life, life itself is gained. The individual does this by having taken the lost image of the loved one into his own concept of himself. Paradoxically, grief must have its work and then life must go on. These two necessities are held in polar tension with each other in the experience of grief. Life undergoes a recentering in the abiding realities of the Eternal, and the shifting unrealities of the temporal are sloughed off. Newer and simpler goals of living are realized and the Beatitudes become realities in the life of the person. He begins finally to know what it means to participate in the resurrection of the Lord Jesus Christ.

An example of this may be drawn from the life of a young Negro man who lost his girl friend's love in a way that pushed him into a severe kind of anxiety of grief. He met his pastor and before he knew it he was telling him all about it. He told his pastor that he was walking about in a daze, and gradually he came to the point where he could accept the fact of her rejection. Then he burst into tears and wept for whole nights at a time. Later as he went about his work, he would suddenly find himself making mistakes because he was thinking of the girl friend he had lost. But recently he said he has found a peace inside, things have become bearable now, he hates that this thing happened, but it is over now, and he feels that he has been " born out of it." He is now trying to find a new purpose for living and feels that as a Christian he has a mission to perform. He is seeking the guidance of a theological professor concerning his plans for further education.

The reader can see that in the preceding paragraph specific reference is made to the Christian experience of grief. At the same time this implies the healthy management of life's inevitable crises. At any point along the way, the process of grief can stalemate, the individual can fixate or regress. Such eventualities lead to the idolatry of the lost love object and a wilting of the religious vitality of the individual. Correspondingly, they lead to the development of the morbid personality wherein the wounds became malignantly destructive. Hence the importance of the anxiety situation of grief both for religion and mental health becomes apparent.

At one state hospital a little, gray-haired mother who has been a patient there for several years comes daily to the office to mail a letter to her son, Eddie. The fact is that Eddie is dead and has been so for years. Yet she writes letters to him regularly. Religious cults have been built upon the unresolved grief of persons whose whole security, i.e., freedom from anxiety of grief, lay in an unrealistic handling of the fact of death. Such was the warning of Jesus to his hearers when he reminded them in the presence of the death of Lazarus that he himself was the resurrection and the life.

IV. Some Biblical Insights Into the Anxiety of Grief

Jesus, as the Suffering Servant, was indeed a " man of sorrows, and acquainted with grief." He confronted a living grief in that " he came to his own home and his own people received him not." He wept over Jerusalem (Matt. 23:37-39; Luke 13:34,35) because of their rejection of him. The central purpose of his ministry, i.e., the bringing of men into the Kingdom of God, had been frustrated by the refusal of the people of Jerusalem to participate with him in his purpose. As Major, Manson, and Wright describe the people of Jerusalem, " they were wedded to things as they were " (op. cit., p. 419). Their rejection of Jesus was epitomized in his trial and condemnation to " suffer outside the gate " of their city; his grief struck its excruciating depths in his cry for forsakenness even from the Father.

The apostle Paul experienced a similar grief over the Israelites' rejection of him and the gospel he preached. He says:

" I have great sorrow and unceasing anguish in my heart. For I could wish that I myself were accursed and cut off from Christ for the sake of my brethren, my kinsmen by race." (Rom. 9:2,3.)

This kind of anguish effectively mirrors the experience of Moses in his intercessory prayer for the Israelites when they had made unto themselves a golden calf for worship. He prayed:

" Alas, this people have sinned a great sin; they have made for themselves gods of gold. But now, if thou wilt forgive their sin — and if not, blot me, I pray thee, out of thy book which thou hast written." (Ex. 32:31,32.)

These three accounts from the Biblical story exemplify the most difficult kind of grief to bear: excommunication by the people whose redemption and healing are one's whole life purpose. Here isolation, separation, and grief concentrate themselves in the personhood of the one sent by God to be sensitive, aware, and prophetic in a community which has become insensitive, callous, and self-seeking. Grief is not usually thought of in connection with such rejection of prophets by their own people, but the processes of grief are plainly evident both from the point of view of the intrapsychic anguish the individual feels and from the point of view of the middle wall of partition erected against him by his coreligionists.

Such processes of this grief are closely associated with the kind of grief a person faces, not upon separation from and rejection by the community he loves, but upon estrangement from or the loss of another individual to whom he is devoted. Turbulent undercurrents of this grief appeared in the experience of Jesus as he looked upon the rich young man and loved him, even though the young man was going away from him sorrowfully. It is seen as Jesus sensed the distance between himself and Judas. Even as he washed the feet of Judas, he sensed the futility of his efforts to sustain the relationship. Likewise, thrusts of grief gripped him over the other disciples' estrangement from him, even in the midst of their loud protestations of fidelity.

Yet, the disciples, in turn, suffered profound bereavement upon the crucifixion of their Lord. They had never perceived him accurately in terms of what his Messiahship really meant. Their materialistic illusions were shattered and the hard reality of the death of Jesus thrust them into despair that sent them back to their fishing. Whereas the anxiety and anguish of Jesus was pure grief, unadulterated with guilt, that of the disciples was coupled with the burden of guilt and sin. They suffered deep remorse which later turned into repentance and a rebirth of the self. In fact the bereavement of the disciples, commingled with guilt over their infidelity to him, was split asunder by the resurrection of our Lord, thereby releasing the outpouring of the power of the Holy Spirit at Pentecost.

The account of the work of the apostles reveals the estrangement of grief again. One of the most graphic examples is the relationship between Barnabas and Paul, particularly as they disagreed over the work of John Mark. (See Acts 15:36–41.) If any investment of relationship has ever been made by one person in another, Barnabas certainly did so with Paul. He invested faith and relationship in a man who had murdered the Christians! He joined Paul as the Christians ordained him as their chief representative to the Gentiles. Now, over Barnabas' like-natured belief and confidence in John Mark " a sharp contention " arose between Barnabas and Paul, and " they separated from each other." What grief Barnabas must have felt! What lonely feelings of estrangement Paul must have felt! Now each of them was on his own. The reference in Col. 4:10 and II Tim. 4:11 seems to indicate that Paul had a change of heart concerning John Mark, and that he later affirmed the worthfulness of John Mark in the Christian enterprise. Nevertheless, the relationship between him and Barnabas, the man who gave him his start in the Christian community, apparently was never the same again. The infection apparently departed and the wound healed but the scar tissues probably remained. A silent testimony to the fact that the conflict did heal over is that there is no record of any sect or cult in early Christianity growing up around Barnabas and/or Paul in such a way as to be in competition with each other. No " root of bitterness " sprang up to defile " the many." Other Christians were not used to perpetuate a personal conflict between the two men.

V. Some Theological Aspects of the Resolution of the Anxiety of Grief

The above account of the experience of Barnabas and Paul provides a good point of departure for a discussion of a pastoral theology of grief. From a theological point of view, the two issues at stake in any grief experience are, first, the temptation to idolatry and, secondly, the shrinking back from the inner appropriation of the power of the resurrection by attempting to avoid the way of the cross.

The temptation to idolatry and the avoidance of the cross as the way to power of the resurrection appear in what is commonly known as "grudge-bearing." The person who bears a grudge toward another has, in a sense, suffered a type of grief. His grudge usually has been preceded by an exceptionally deep and overdependent friendship. In this sense, the proverb that familiarity breeds contempt is true. But when a deep rift comes in such a familiar relationship, violent hostility emerges and may settle down into a permanent pattern of grudge-bearing. The temptation to idolatry here is great in that the person against whom the grudge is borne takes the place of God in the grudge bearer's life. Soon the grudge bearer ceases to pray and begins to be consumed by his own wrath toward the other person. (Hence, the importance of praying for one's enemies cannot be overestimated.) The end extreme of this condition is apparent in the paranoid individual whose feelings of persecution are highly organized around one individual or a group of persons. This is all that 'he can think about consciously, and everything stands in reference to these plotters who are trying to do him harm.

The way of the cross with reference to these settled antipathies is set forth in Jesus' teachings about forgiveness, and the pattern of reconciliation set forth in Matt. 18:15-17:

"If your brother sins against you, go and tell him his fault, between you and him alone. If he listens to you, you have gained your brother.

But if he does not listen, take one or two others along with you, that every word may be confirmed by the evidence of two or three witnesses. If he refuses to listen to them, tell it to the church; and if he refuses to listen even to the church, let him be to you as a Gentile and a tax collector."

To consider someone as a Gentile, as a heathenish person, is really to place him among the idolaters who worship at a pagan shrine. This is the judgment of Jesus upon the unforgiving and irreconcilable person: he is an idolater and should be considered so. If he chooses to participate in the pathological realm of evil spirits, one should not also participate with him. The only antidote for him is that he cast down every high thing or "proud obstacle" that exalts itself against the knowledge of God, and that he bring every thought into "captivity" to the Lordship of Jesus. The churches are replete with persons who carry these private crosses and endure these inner griefs and no account of grief and its resolution is complete without having taken cognizance of them.

The temptation to idolatry in grief appears when the grief-stricken person begins to organize his permanent way of life around the grief situation. This is especially true when the loss of the loved one is caused by death. For instance, Auguste Comte actually made an altar of the chair in which his Clotilde sat before her death. He developed an elaborate worship ritual and gathered a small sect of followers to idolize her also. A grief-stricken mother may organize the whole family around a continual worship of the memory of a son killed in the war, neglecting the needs of the other children who are alive with her. A father, bitter because his prayers for his daughter's recovery were not answered, may cease to go to church, cease to educate his children religiously, and refuse to participate with his wife in family worship. This may very easily be a temporary stage in the grief process. But such an attitude may also become a kind of idolatry when the person adopts it as a more or less permanent pattern of life. The poignant aspect of such a temptation to idolatry was expressed by a doctor to the father of a small boy who was about to die. The young father said to the doctor: " You just must save this baby. He is all there is to us." The doctor replied, " My son, the good book says, ' Thou shalt have no other gods before me '! "

The idolatry of the dead is the most deceptive and subtle kind of idolatry because it can so easily clothe itself in Christian symbols. At this point, religious teachings that tend to gloss over the fact of death, as well as the extreme use of artificiality by some morticians today, tend to aid and abet the idolatrous needs of the grief-stricken.

Jesus sensed the need of his disciples to depreciate the fact of death in that he told them plainly that Lazarus was dead. He told them that he was glad that he was not present at the dying of his friend in order that they might believe. The sisters of Lazarus apparently had the same shallow belief in Jesus in that they also said that if he had been present there would have been no such thing as a death. They had fixed their hope upon him as one who would enable all to avoid the fact of death, but the reality of death is reiterated in the Johannine account when it records that the odor of death was apparent in the corpse of four days.

On the other hand, Jesus sensed the sisters' need to idolize Lazarus to the exclusion of higher loyalty to him as Lord and to the Kingdom of God as the purpose of life. His raising of Lazarus relocated their loyalty to the proper center of their being and saved them from idolatry. This, it seems, is the significance of his conversation with Martha:

" ' And even now I know that whatever you ask from God, God will give you.' Jesus said to her, ' Your brother will rise again.' Martha said to him, ' I know that he will rise again in the resurrection at the last day.' Jesus said to her, ' I am the resurrection and the life; he who believes in me, though he die, yet shall he live, and whoever lives and believes in me shall never die. Do you believe this? ' She said to him, ' Yes, Lord; I believe that you are the Christ, the Son of God, he who is coming into the world.' " (John 11:22–27.)

Inherent in these teachings is an antidote for all teaching that would make death seem like something else and substitute an idolatry of the dead for faith in the living God. The death of Jesus himself was real, and he did not simply enact a drama that made him seem to die. He was crucified in the flesh, and it was a real death he died. Contemporary unrealism about death is based upon a gnostic approach to life and ensues in different types of cults of healing and spiritualism which depend upon an emaciated sorcery rather than a red-blooded participation in the way of the cross as a way of life. Such participation identifies the way of the cross with the ongoing power of life itself and though an individual is " killed all the day long," the inner man is " renewed everyday " as he looks " not to the things that are seen but to the things that are unseen; for the things that are seen are transient, but the things that are unseen are eternal " (II Cor. 4:18).

CHAPTER

4

THE ANXIETY OF SIN

I. THE FACTUALITY OF SIN

Hans Trub, in an article entitled "Individuation, Guilt and Decision," tells of one of his own personal experiences which he calls an "appearance of an absolute phenomenon of guilt." He says that he felt guilt in such a way as to call it an "endless total fall" and of having "fallen into guilt." Out of the depths of this guilt consciousness, he anxiously accepted himself as a responsible person before God and was able to say: "Here I stand guilty, and I take upon myself responsibility for my guilt. Here is my guilt that cannot be explained away, and in this moment of confession and admission I know clearly that an 'I myself' exists, and I stand on firm ground." (*Die kulturelle Bedentung der komplexen Psychologie,* 1935; quoted in Göte Bergston, *Pastoral Psychology,* p. 151. The Macmillan Company, 1951.)

Counselors and psychotherapists recognize the feelings expressed so powerfully by Milton:

> "And like a devilish engine back recoils
> Upon himself. Horror and doubt distract
> His troubled thoughts, and from the bottom stir
> The hell within him. . . .
> "Now conscience wakes despair
> That slumbered; wakes the bitter memory
> Of what he was, what is, and what must be
> Worse; of worse deeds worse sufferings must ensue!"
> (Milton, *Paradise Lost,* Book IV.)

Much that has been said or done in the area of counseling and psychotherapy, however, seems to have been based upon the hope

of resolving guilt as something that is always symptomatic of
other things and not real in itself. Such an attitude does not
draw a distinction between guilt and sin. For this reason psychotherapeutic literature has very few specific discussions of the anxiety of sin, per se. Vander Veldt and Odenwald, writing on "Psychiatry and Catholicism," naturally are exceptions to this. They
say:

"Sin and guilt do not parallel each other.
Sin is a violation of the moral law and, therefore, an offense against
the supreme Lawgiver. Sin supposes full consciousness." (James H.
Vander Veldt and Robert P. Odenwald, *Psychiatry and Catholicism*,
p. 187. McGraw-Hill Book Company, Inc., 1952.)

The brunt of such reason apparently is that the person who knows
to do right and does it not, to him it is sin. Obviously the capacity
to sin represents a relatively high state of moral development
and the anxiety of sin is a normal type of anxiety.

When Trub underscores the necessity of taking his stand with
guilt at some point of reality for which he himself is personally
responsible before God and at a point beyond which he need
look no farther, he affirms the fact that there is a point at which
guilt becomes sin. Sin is that guilt for which one must needs
accept personal responsibility. Of course, such a stand is not to
discount the tributaries of motivation that flow into the acts of
one's life. It is to say, however, that the insight gained by analysis is subsidiary to that gained by accepting oneself as a sinner
before God. At their risk of total destruction, the sinner bears
his heart before God and enters the forgiveness which reveals
to him that he is acceptable to God *though unacceptable even
to himself.* This is the anxiety of sin.

Nathaniel Hawthorne, in *The Scarlet Letter,* tells of a minister
who stood on the "very proudest pre-eminence of superiority"
with a "reputation of white sanctity" and a "professional character"—"itself a lofty pedestal." He had committed adultery
with a woman who was cast out for her sin which she confessed
through the birth of his child. She chose to shield him and not
to confess for him. The minister carried the brand of his sin

inside his shirt; she carried hers on her forehead. The minister chose to confide his secret to a lecherous counselor, Roger Chillingworth, who exploited him with this secret knowledge about him, seeking to work revenge on him for his good favor in the sight of the woman he loved. Finally, the minister was goaded to a public confession of his sin, and as a miserable offender died in his act of confession. Because his counselor betrayed him and used him for revenge, he had no interpreter of his sin before his own eyes and no interlocutor between him and the community. As he died, he said to his counselor: " May God forgive thee! Thou, too, hast deeply sinned! "

The pastoral counselor, particularly, is out of touch with his true destiny as a minister if he does not subordinate all his concerns to his ministry of reconciliation through the forgiveness of sins by God. When he is at home in this sense of destiny, he discovers that his colleagues in the field of psychotherapy have a clear ground of understanding with him.

For instance, an abundance of clinical experience validates this approach to the needs of unhappy persons. A psychiatrist referred one of his patients to the author. He said that the reason he did so was that she felt condemned and separated from God for having done things that she really should have felt guilty for having done. He did not choose to give her an " out " for her sense of sin, but inasmuch as his psychotherapy had brought it into conscious awareness, and inasmuch as she felt the need for the forgiveness of God, he referred her to a minister for instruction in the forgiveness of God.

A young couple had sought repeatedly to get married. On three occasions the bride-to-be had broken the plans because of an illness. She began to sense the illness to be allied with her reluctance to leave home. In the process of pastoral counseling, the depths of her sense of disloyalty to her father in getting married surfaced. She did not feel that she could possibly be doing the will of God to leave her father to be constantly slandered by her mother. She and her father had always been joined in a common cause of protecting each other from the unfairness of a mentally sick mother who was constantly accusing the father of dishonesty, unfaithfulness, etc. As the girl began to get free of her sense of sin, the pressure of her illness was relieved. In the impending possibility that a lung disorder would recur, she sought premarital pastoral counseling. In the discovery of her sense of sin, in an enlarged perception of the will of God, and in the fellowship of a Christian group she discovered relief and redirection. She did not become ill; she clarified her intention to marry; she has had no recurrence of the illness in eight years.

An irate husband came to his pastor almost dragging his young wife by the arm. She confessed, at her husband's insistence, to having been out several times with another man. She said she could no longer feel any love for either of them, though, and chose to separate herself from both of them. In her private conversations later with the pastor, she said she could no longer pray, that God seemed very far away from her, and that her prayers got no higher than the ceiling.

A prominent financial leader became secretly involved in the diverting of funds. His organization had such complete confidence in him that they did not check his books closely to see what he was doing. He became addicted to the embezzlement and a little more was taken each time. He finally bore the weight of his sin as long as he could; he told it and took a prison sentence. He said that he felt good and clean for the first time in years. The person who had been stealing all those years did not even seem like himself, it was a " not me," and now he was glad to be reunited with himself.

A successful lawyer had yearned for years for a certain political position. He had striven with many opponents and had ruthlessly walked over many people in his quest for power. Now, at the sudden, unexpected death of one of his political partners, he was, by an involved series of office shifts, given the position without any effort on his part. He was overcome with an unreasonable depression. He came to his minister with a long confession of contrition over the many " deals " in which he had been involved.

A young businessman went to one of his immediate superiors who happened also to be a lay reader in the Episcopal church in his community. He began to tell him of a vague sense of uneasiness that kept him from doing his work and said that there were some personal confidences he wanted to share with his boss, but that he felt that he should go to a psychiatrist instead. His reason for this was that the psychiatrist could give him absolute confidential healing, whereas the privileged communication he wished to share would complicate his other relationships to his boss and lay reader friend. The friend referred him to a psychiatrist, who in turn said that the person should return to a minister for help. The psychiatrist felt that the problems — involving extramarital relationships — were of such a nature as to warrant a confessional ministry and not psychiatric treatment.

In all these cases and in many others the quality and direction of anxiety determine the way in which sin manifests itself in human behavior. Therefore, anxiety conditions also the way in which the pastoral counselor deals with the sense of sin. The next two chapters, one on compulsive or legalistic anxiety and the other on the absence of anxiety, will further clarify this concept. In the anxiety of sin, however, the amount and quality of anxiety are directly and accurately in proportion to the real inner motives of the sinner. He sees himself as he really is and is genuinely grieved because his low estimate of himself is an established fact. The problem of the pastoral counselor is to understand the process of this grief, the constructive and destructive directions of the anxiety the person expresses, and the ways in which this anxiety may be mobilized toward the relief of the person through confession, self-dedication, and the grace of God.

II. THE PROCESS OF THE ANXIETY OF SIN

The study of the anxiety of grief in the previous chapter is a helpful guide in understanding the process of the anxiety of sin. In fact, the anxiety of sin is a special type of grief situation in that the individual is separated and estranged from his meaningful community by his sin. He has lost communication with those who mean most to him, and this is true even in terms of his relationship to God. As one person in a confessional situation said, "It does not even seem that God is there any more." A careful look at this process of separation and estrangement reveals the painful uneasiness of mind which it creates in a sinner.

1. *The isolating power of sin.* Sin always appears in terms of disrupted interpersonal relationships. From the pattern of these interpersonal relationships, sin draws its meaning and interpretation and exacts its penalty and punishment. A comparison of the anxiety of grief to the anxiety of sin throws light on the dark activity of the sin-laden mind. The anxiety of grief is the reaction of a person to a significant and meaningful loss. The anxiety of sin is the reaction of a person to *being* lost, to having lost his way, his meaning, his purpose, his *raison d'être*. Likewise, his way, his meaning, his purpose, his *raison d'être* arise from his sense of community with and acceptance by those whom he loves, to whom he is devoted, and from whom he gains his resources for living. The anxiety of sin and condemnation therefore arises from estrangement and alienation from one's total field of interpersonal relationships — to his community, to his God, and to himself. His sinful acts are both caused by and contributed to by widening chasms of alienation between him and his enduring community: his family, his church, his work group, his God, and his concept of himself. He is caught in a vicious circle of rejection and rebellion. He is "cut off from the land of the living."

Examples of this isolation are evident in the New Testament: the anxiety of sin strikes with the power to kill in such experiences of Ananias and Sapphira. They deceived the community of early Christians. This was their sin. They broke relationship with the community of the Jews in order to cast their lot with the Christians. However, they could not *wholly* give themselves to the Christian fellowship. That uncommunicated part of themselves became the festering point of their anxiety of sin. When the full brunt of their alienation, and the real sin which occasioned it, struck them, they died. The anxiety of this estrangement was too much for them to bear.

This is the exact opposite of the anxiety of grief which Jesus bore, which resulted in his death on the cross. The difference between the death of Jesus and the death of Ananias and Sapphira illustrates catastrophically the difference between the anxiety of grief, on the one hand, and the anxiety of sin on the other. The end result of death was the same, but the driving force of the anxiety was quite different. (Sometimes the anxiety of grief such as Jesus experienced is taken up by a paranoid person who is burdened within with the anxiety of sin. Yet he consciously perceives himself as free from sin, perfect in every way, and as actually the Saviour of the world, in his own eyes, to say the least.)

2. *The power of excommunication.* The estrangement and alienation characteristic of sin naturally is also rooted in the need of the community to defend itself from the sinner. The sinner both cuts himself off from and is cut off by the community, i.e., the land of the living. The community's defensiveness makes it difficult for the sinner to understand the source of his own sinfulness, even as it also makes it difficult for the so-called respectable person properly to locate the motive for his righteousness. This anxiety distorts the sense of sin and makes it difficult for the sinner to find forgiveness even from God. It stands to reason that if the community would not forgive the individual for his failings and stumblings, his inner certainty of God's forgiveness would never be quite secure. Yet the community is made up of human beings whose acceptance also has its limits.

Consequently, the sinner must find some way of establishing communication with the people with whom he lives and moves and has his being. Experience teaches a variety of ways whereby sin-laden men establish this communication with the fellowship of Christians, thereby finding relief from the anxiety of sin and security in the communion of the people of God. These ways of establishing communication with the anxious sinner need description:

a. For instance, in the Old Testament account, cities of refuge were established wherein the offender of the community might both receive protection from avengers and at the same time stay in touch with "the congregation" for a wise and just decision concerning his offense (Num. 35:9 ff.). In modern society, Alcoholics Anonymous is something of a "city of refuge" for the person whose plight alienates him from others, yet who cannot be healed apart from a meaningful community. Similarly, divorcees, ex-convicts, and more recently recovered mental patients, who are somewhat excommunicated by their communities, are beginning to find fellowship with each other in their sufferings in groups similar to Alcoholics Anonymous.

b. Another example of the way in which persons bearing the anxiety of sin establish communication with the larger fellowship of healing helpfulness is through *symbolic acts*. Many burn themselves out in propitiatory service to the community, hoping to merit the approval of the community if indeed they should be found out for their weaknesses. Yet they bear the burden also of fear lest they be found out for what they are and the burden of unworthiness inasmuch as they feel that they are deceptively appearing to be something they are not. Such suffering is seen in the convert disobedience of the Morality Act by the hero of Alan Paton's novel *Too Late the Phalarope*. Finally he was discovered by an enemy who jealously hungered for his destruction. The author says in commenting upon the calamity: "So we were all struck down. Because he would not tell one man, therefore the whole world knew" (p. 267; Charles Scribner's Sons, 1953).

An unmarried woman of twenty-eight years of age, for example, felt profound shame over her ignoble birth. She was a person who tended to accept personal responsibility for other people's acts rather than her own. She was anxious over their sin, not her own. She could never communicate her sense of unworthiness, but she acted it out in her various places of employment by telling elaborate stories of how respected, wealthy, and venerable were her family and ancestors. Then she had to forge checks to keep up the impression she had created. When she began to clarify her motives for these symbolic acts, they were no longer necessary, inasmuch as she had established a secure and accepting relationship to her pastor and through him to the community as a whole.

c. The fellowship of confession in the community of the church provides a sound ground of communication of the anxiety of sin. Only recently have Protestants begun to perceive anew that the need to confess one's faults to one another in the Christian community in order that one may be healed is not a violation of faith in God's power to forgive. Rather it manifests God's love through his revelation of himself in Christ and through the record of that revelation in the Bible, but also through embodiment of that grace in the accepting and relieving love of one's fellow human beings. Yet, even as sin involves risk as it abounds, grace involves more risk. The church community that operates purely upon a morality of safety inevitably is a legalistic community. It quickly breaks communication with its members at the slightest appearance of rebellion, excommunicating the sinner in order to defend itself. Jesus operated far out beyond the boundaries of the safe confines of Pharisaism, risking destruction from both the sinful and the righteous.

The Holy Spirit produces the awareness of broken communication as men in the anxiety of their sin build one Tower of Babel after another and lose touch with all that is real in the process. This awareness produces both the anxiety of grief and of sin. In turn, the Holy Spirit develops that kind of understanding community between men whereby they may reveal their real selves to each other without being destroyed. In other words, the processes of forgiveness operate apace with the processes of repentance. The fruit of the Spirit, therefore, is the courage of confession in the sinner and the courage of acceptance and forgiveness in the church.

The courage of confession is the antithesis of the anxiety of sin and actually overcomes it in several different ways: First, the lay members of churches are often spiritually understanding of each other's sins. In a real sense, the anxiety of sin is a fellowship in that all have sinned and come short of the grace of God. For instance, a young woman in a small church was reported to have stolen some money from her employers and to have been discharged for that reason. She kept her troubles to herself for some time, but when she finally did choose to communicate her distress, she went to the owner of the general store in which her husband was employed. He received her confession with wisdom and confidence, and heard her pour out her anxiety of sin before God. He did not attempt to remove the consequences of her sin, but wisely began to develop an understanding pattern of action whereby she might follow up her repentance with restitution and whereby she might be protected from isolation and unnecessary ridicule in the community. Her church was her main bulwark in enabling her to learn from experience and to understand her own actions.

In the second place, the courage of confession overcomes the anxiety of sin in the fellowship of the church by the willingness of Christians to admonish or rebuke one another in the frankness of transparent love. If the genial friend of the hero of Paton's *Too Late the Phalarope* who operated the tobacco store could have broken through the barrier of the anxiety of sin to encourage him toward confidence in some member of the community, the man could have been helped earlier.

In the third place, those burdened with the anxiety of sin are encouraged to confession by the skill of pastors whose primary art should lie in enabling the sin-laden to express their anxiety over their sins. Persons with a condemning heart, ignorant of the ways of God, have access to the community as a whole in the personhood of the minister in that he actually represents the community. He is a minister of reconciliation, not only between the sinner and God, but also between the sinner and the community. If he presumes to speak personally to the individual, he should identify his opinion as his own otherwise he will build an expectancy on the part of the confessing person of the same attitude from the whole church. The minister is always caught between the ninety-nine and the one in such instances, and should never forget that he is the shepherd of the whole flock.

III. The Anxiety of Sin and Inner Confession

The cleavages of communication involved in the anxiety of guilt involve more than a painful uneasiness of mind over separation and estrangement from the community, however. A grief situation exists *within* the individual himself: he is grieved for his shattered ideal of himself. The illusion of his perfection and the integrity of his confidence for not having sinned are gone. The process of grief moves through the stages which have already been described. The shock of having done that which is evil is there: " What a terrible thing to do! " The numbness of realization follows: " I cannot imagine that I could have done such a thing! It seems like a horrible dream! " The struggle between fantasy and reality continues the inner conflict: " Shall I think back over this in the illusion that it was perfectly right and thoroughly justified, and thereby enjoy the sin again in fantasy? " The break-through of a flood of grief comes: " I have sinned! Things will never be the same again! Life is no longer worth living." Grief work revamps the whole self-concept, and through repentance and restitution the individual finds forgiveness and restoration — or he does not!

The turning point of this inner grief situation impinges upon whether or not the individual can accept himself after having received the forgiveness of God and his community. He may choose to worship the idol of his former self, the self he imagines himself to be. He may, as did Jacob, refuse to be comforted because of his own guilt in the loss of Joseph. He may even come up with the pathological anxiety (which will be described later) of having committed the unpardonable sin. Deep inner distortions of personality plague this person, and he truly has need of a physician as well as of the divine. Nevertheless, such an understanding of the processes of grief and guilt is prerequisite to an adequate therapy.

IV. The Difference Between the Anxiety of Grief and the Anxiety of Sin

The point has been made that the anxiety of grief and the anxiety of sin have certain vital realities in common. However, this is not to make them identical. In even more vital ways they are quite different.

For instance, it would be very easy to assume from what has been said about Jesus' having experienced the anxiety of grief that he was involved in the experience of sin. But to do so would be to miss the point of the basic differences between the anxiety of grief and the anxiety of sin. These need to be clarified here.

The anxiety of grief differs essentially from the anxiety of sin in that its sources are different. Usually both of them arise out of disruptions of interpersonal relationships, but the disruption in the case of grief is rooted in love and in the case of sin is rooted in hostility and fear. Furthermore, grief has its source in a yearning movement toward and with persons, whereas sin is derived from an antipathetic movement against persons or a recalcitrant withdrawal from persons.

In the second place, the anxiety of grief differs from the anxiety of sin in a qualitative way. For instance, pure grief, unalloyed with the anxiety of sin and grief, is a qualitative *helpless* experience in that the grief-stricken person can actually *do nothing* about his loss. On the other hand, the sin-laden person has the alternative of confession and restitution; he can actually *do something* about his situation, even though the problem of communication is more acute for him.

At this point, grief is qualitatively different from sin in that it is more communicable and socially acceptable, and the individual receives more community support and participation in his attempts to manage the anxiety involved. The community in many types of grief situations has ritualized its supportive ministry into specific customs, such as the visitation of the bereaved and the sick. To the contrary, the sin-laden individual is isolated, ostracized, and excommunicated. Only in the redemptive grief of the prophets do parallels between the anxiety of grief and the anxiety of sin begin to form. Could this be what was meant when it is said that the One who knew no sin was made to be sin in man's behalf?

Finally, the anxiety of grief and the anxiety of sin differ in the effects they work in the structure and behavioral function of the personality. The anxiety of grief does not call for as many defensive mechanisms of personality — such as rationalization, projection, reaction formations, and displacements — as does the anxiety of sin. The inner springs of insight are more often opened by the anxiety of grief and more often closed by the anxiety of sin. As a result, the effects of sin are more often disintegrating and defensive whereas the effects of the anxiety of grief are more often distilling and integrative. The anxiety of grief mellows; the anxiety of sin may harden.

These are somewhat arbitrary distinctions for the simple reason that in the human situation grief and sin, as has already been pointed out, rarely if ever appear in isolation from each other. Nevertheless, they do appear in such full force of their separate characters as to be seen in relatively unalloyed forms. Seeing them thus clarifies their basic differences.

V. The Cross and the Anxiety of Sin

The anxiety of sin springs from the enchantment of sin, and the enchantment of sin is broken through the greater power of the cross. The Biblical statement of this appears in the exhortation of Heb. 12:1,2:

"Let us also lay aside every weight, and sin which clings so closely, and let us run with perseverance the race that is set before us, looking to Jesus the pioneer and perfecter of our faith, who for the joy that was set before him endured the cross, despising the shame, and is seated at the right hand of the throne of God."

The anxiety of sin is the "sickness unto death," as Sören Kierkegaard has called it. He says that in "Christian terminol-

ogy death is the expression for the greatest spiritual wretchedness" (*The Sickness Unto Death,* p. 4). As Paul put it:
" Wretched man that I am! Who will deliver me from this body
of death? " (Rom. 7:24). In speaking of the healing of the sickness unto death, Kierkegaard again says, " The cure is simply
to die, to ' die from.' " This dying from sin is actually a dying *to*
sin, as Paul again says, " How can we who died to sin still live
in it? " This dying from sin to sin is the Christian experience of
the cross of Jesus. The apostle Paul related the anxiety of sin to
personal participation in the cross of Jesus in three vivid pictures
in the sixth chapter of Romans. He said that the person who had
died to sin could no longer live therein. His first picture was that
of the death, burial, and resurrection of Jesus as symbolized in
baptism:

" We were buried therefore with him by baptism into death, so that
as Christ was raised from the dead by the glory of the Father, we too
might walk in newness of life " (Rom. 6:4).

Paul's second picture was that of the planting or uniting with
him in *a death like his,* and participation with him in a resurrection like his. This picture is reminiscent of the Johannine
thought, " Unless a grain of wheat falls into the earth and dies,
it remains alone." Here is a symbolic description of the aloneness,
or isolation of the life, which holds itself back for itself and away
from the fellowship of participation in the way of the cross. The
egocentric nature of sin, always calling attention to the self as
the center of existence, is challenged by the losing of life in order
to save life. Each of the cases presented in this discussion of the
anxiety of sin may be considered in this light with valuable in-
terpretative results.

The final picture that Paul presents is that of the crucifixion
itself:

" We know that our old self was crucified with him so that the sinful
body might be destroyed, and we might no longer be enslaved to sin.
For he who died is freed from sin." (Rom. 6:6,7.)

LEGALISTIC ANXIETY

I. SPIRITUAL EXTERNALISM AND DISTORTIONS OF THE CONSCIENCE

A shopworker consulted the author in a Southern city about the unhappiness of his seven-year-old daughter. He started his conversation by saying, " You see she's got an unnecessary conscience." When asked what he meant by an unnecessary conscience, he said: " She feels bad about doing little wrong things more than it's necessary for anybody to hate themselves that way. She will take a small piece of chalk from the blackboard at school and bring it home. When she gets home, she hands it to us and tells us how awful she is for being so mean. She cries and won't eat her supper and asks us to pray for her. I think that's an unnecessary conscience." The author, after careful and sympathetic hearing of the whole story, encouraged the father to take his daughter to the local child guidance clinic, because the child apparently needed very careful attention by someone who would be near her over a period of time.

The anxiety of sin is that kind of anxiety in which the sense of personal responsibility is in ethical perspective with the actual deeds done by the person. However, such an unnecessary conscience calls attention to the fact, as do those that follow in these pages, that the anxiety of a person may be completely out of focus with the reality to which they attach their sense of guilt. The psychotherapists rightly call attention to the legalistic nature of this anxiety, the way in which the scrupulosity of a person may distort radically the ethical perspective of the individual. This condition presents a "disrelationship" between the anxiety and the guilt, and may rightly be called legalistic anxiety, or the anxiety of the minutiae of the law. Many other clinical examples of this kind of anxiety, drawn from actual counseling situations in the parish ministry, serve to illustrate this kind of anxiety in people.

A mother called her pastor and asked if he would be willing to talk with her child. She said she had scolded him for his bad habits but it did not seem to do any good. She said he played with his sexual parts and it seemed that telling him what a sin it was did not seem to mean anything to him, and she had heard that this would affect his mind and felt that she needed to get him some help before it ruined him forever. The pastor carefully encouraged the mother to tell him more of the troubles she had been having with the child. She was a very religious mother who wanted her child to be perfect before the Lord, as she put it. She wanted him to grow up to be a servant of God, and felt that these habits were an offense to God. The pastor dealt with her several times in giving her religious re-education, but he also sought the help of the local child guidance clinic in bringing a more stable kind of mental health to the mother and child, and in developing a more considerate attitude on the part of the father for the mother.

Pastors repeatedly talk with persons who are convinced that they are lost and nothing can be done to save them. They may tell the pastor that they have committed the unpardonable sin, and that they are beyond redemption. They scrupulously study authoritarian statements of faith, seeking a final answer to all their anxieties. In the initial conversation with them it should be routine practice to discover the other counselors to whom they have been. Repeatedly these persons tell of one authoritarian person after another whom they have consulted. The course of their conversations with other counselors reveal that they compulsively demand a *legal formula* whereby they might be relieved of anxiety of destruction without any particular changes in their own demanding natures. An undercurrent of defiance was felt in their attitude toward their counselors. It was as if they were asking their religious guides to be their idols in order that they in turn might desecrate them. These taunting relationships usually ended in the loss of patience on the part of the counselor and a subsequent referral that often was perceived as rejection by the counselee.

Such a person should be firmly told that his particular need for salvation calls for an inner kind of release from bondage and that no formula will magically save him. Rather, a pastor should develop a series of spiritual conversations over a period of time in order to become a meaningful friend to him. Whereas no specific formula is available for his particular complaint a pastor can afford him some time in working with him as he learns the meaning and purpose of life. If he would like to develop such an ordered and disciplined friendship, he might discover more about life than what the unpardonable sin is. If he carries through with such a challenge, a pastor can strengthen his religious security as the flexibility of the friendship overcomes some of his fears and casts out some of his apprehensiveness. In instances where specific acts underlie the feeling of having committed the unpardonable sin a confessional relationship usually clears the anxiety.

A rather complete account of the poignant suffering and inner distress of such a person is recorded in the following clinical account of a series of interviews with a patient in a general medical and surgical hospital:

On May 4, 1946, a young woman, twenty-eight years of age, was called to the chaplain's attention by the hospital hostess. The patient had told the hostess that she could not feel that she was saved, although she had been saved at one time. The hostess said that the chaplain should visit her after having herself spoken of the doctrine of the "once saved always saved."

The chaplain found the patient very friendly. A good understanding grew very easily and the patient readily gave the following information about herself. She is living on a farm with her husband and eight-year-old boy. She has been to a sanatorium for tubercular patients and found it very lonely there. She has come here for a lobectomy. She finds the nurses very helpful, and a homelike atmosphere in the hospital. After a few superficial remarks the chaplain handed her a devotional booklet that had in it a group of prayers and Scripture passages.

The patient immediately began to talk of her religious life. She said that she would not mind this operation so very much if she felt that she was saved. She said that she was a member of a Baptist Church, but that she did not feel that she was saved. Mrs. B, the hostess, had talked with her about it and seemed to think that if she were once saved, she would always be saved, but she could not get that feeling. She said that she was converted when she was sixteen, but that she felt right for only a little while, and that wore off. Now, she says: "I feel like I am not saved and can't get any other feeling. I keep telling myself that God is good and that he is forgiving, but I can't feel that he feels that way toward me."

The chaplain replied: "You were converted when you were sixteen. Would you like to go back and tell me about that conversion experience?" Without hesitation the patient told the following story: "I was converted in the early spring: March it was. I felt like I should go up and ask for Baptism. I felt all right for a while, but there is something in my life that I can't get out, and now every time I think about God, that comes between me. I don't believe that you can be saved and have something between you and God all the time. This is a thing that I was not responsible for; someone else did it to me, but I can't get it off my mind. I keep trying to push it out of my mind, all right, but when I think of God it always comes right back. The thing this person did to me has come between me and my mother and we are not the same that we were before it happened."

"Then it came between you and your mother?"

"Yes, we never talk about it, but it is there and things have never been the same. You see, it is with reference to my stepfather. It all began when I was about nine years old. My father and mother were divorced when I was five years old. He was cruel to her, and she divorced him. She married my stepfather when I was nine years old and shortly afterward, this thing happened. By now, I guess, you are aware of what it was."

The chaplain said: "I presume it was something suggestive between you and your stepfather. Feel free to talk about it if you like and don't feel that you must if you don't care to do so."

The patient continued: " Well, it never got beyond suggestion. I fought him and screamed when he would come near me. Every time Mother would turn her back, he would be making passes at me. At night I was constantly afraid that he would come in on me. I would scream and run out of the room when he would come near me, and go tell my mother, but she did not want to believe me. She never believed. Things were not the same between me and my mother after this. This went on from the time I was nine until I was sixteen. Then something terrible happened. In December before I was converted in March, he was killed in a mine accident. He was supposedly a good man in the community and everyone thought a lot of him. He died a hero's death, strangely enough. He died trying to save another fellow's life. I can't say that I am not glad that he is dead. I think that a person can't feel the way I felt about his death and still be saved. The Bible says that no murderer can get into the Kingdom. And it is as though I killed him myself, because I am glad that he is dead. And my mother thinks now that he was the guilty one in his feeling toward me. She came back after the mine accident and the first thing that she said to me after I saw her was, ' Then he did do it to you and it is true, isn't it? ' But still things have never been the same between us.

" The things between us had gone on for years, and I had never realized that he could have been prosecuted legally for what he was trying to do to me until I had one of my boy friends tell me that he was wise to my stepfather, and that he could be put in the pen for what he was trying to do. I went on back — it was on Sunday morning after church — I went on back home. I saw him and told him that if he ever laid a hand on me again I was going to call the law. It was the last time that he bothered me. It was not long after that that he was killed."

The patient suggested that she felt that he might have had some thought of his wrong there in those last few moments before he was killed and that God might have saved him. Then she went on to tell that she had felt that he had her charmed and that she would be under his spell. She says that even now as she thinks about him she thinks of what a fine man he could have been and what a fine man everyone else but her thought he was. She just let people go on feeling the way they did about him and did not try to change their feelings, because they would never have believed her. She keeps these things out of her mind all she can, but she says that they come pushing back. She will go along all right for five or six days and then all of a sudden she will see some man that looks like him, that walks like him, or combs his hair like him, and then it will all come back to her. (As the patient says this there is a sort of " charmed " look, a faraway gaze, in her eyes.)

The patient went on to say that she was married when she was eighteen. Her husband and she did not get along well at all. She felt all the time the cloud of this thing hanging over her. She conceived and their child was born about two years after their marriage. But her husband became alcoholic and she was forced to divorce him. She went on for a couple of years and met her present husband. She says that her present husband is a wonderful person to her little boy. They live on a farm outside the city and the patient is devotedly in love with him. He gives her security and kindness, and cares for her child as though it were his. This raises another guilt in her mind: that of her divorce. She says that the Bible teaches that remarriage is adultery. She has always been taught this. The patient says that her mother before her was divorced and that she often feels herself being drawn into the same sort of life that was her mother's. She says for that reason she is glad that her child is a little boy and not a girl. Then turning with a sort of helplessness, she asked the chaplain: " Now what is right? Is it a sin to be remarried? If I am to be right with God, does that mean that I would have to tear down all that is good and right in my relation to D [her husband]? "

The chaplain said that life cannot be thrown into reverse so easily as all that. God in his judgment looks upon the causes of divorce more than he does upon divorce itself, and his judgment is in the form not of condemnation but of understanding, intelligence, and love. The chaplain continued by saying that God expects the repentant person to make restitution where it is possible and takes his sincere repentance as sufficient for the errors of the past that cannot be restored. The chaplain added that it was apparent that the first marriage had little of love and little of Christ in it, and that a sincere rededication of life was the requirement of God and that genuine repentance was prerequisite to that.

The patient seemed relieved and said that she wanted to feel the approval of God, but could not possibly see how it would be right to destroy the love relationship between her and her husband who loved her and her little boy so much. The chaplain agreed that it seemed impossible and said that he felt that it was unnecessary.

Then the patient came back to the guilt she felt concerning her feelings toward her stepfather. She says that she can't seem to get release from the fear she has that the thoughts of that will come back on her. The chaplain suggested that if she could restore the relationship between her and her mother through talking the thing out with her mother in an understanding sort of way, she would gradually begin to lose the sense of alienation from God. When a person is at variance with people it is difficult to feel at one with God. God is Christ-like and says, " Neither do I condemn you."

The patient talked again about the fretful time she has had over her feeling about her stepfather. She says that she has never had anyone to tell about it.

The chaplain suggested that he thought that she had talked a lot, but that he would like to continue at another time so that she would not be so tired. The patient said that she had heard about Catholics who went to their priests and shared their problems with them. " I think that I will use you like that! " (Very enthusiastic and elated.)

May 5/46. The patient was agitated because of drug reaction, and was too sick to talk. She was excited about a blood donor needed at the last moment, but the chaplain said he would get one for her. He then had prayer and read the 103d Psalm. The patient said, " I don't know what I would have done had I not come here."

May 6/46. The patient is going to the operating room and asks for prayer. She knows her condition is serious.

May 7/46. The patient is under an oxygen tent and is gasping for breath. She has contracted pneumonia in the lung and is fearful that she is going to die. She says that she has done all she can to get well and somebody had better do something if she's to get any better. The patient grasped for the hand of the chaplain on the top of the oxygen tent cover. She gasped, " Please read the Twenty-third Psalm." The chaplain did and prayed a brief prayer.

May 8/46. The patient is still in the same condition as described above. The chaplain follows much the same procedure.

May 9/46. The patient died at 11:00 P.M.

This patient received an abiding sense of forgiveness and reconciliation, it seemed to the chaplain, as he read the 103d Psalm to her. However, a pastor can have some dismal failures in dealing with such persons in that the counselees actually felt God to have left them in their lostness and feelings of unworthiness of God's love. They in turn feel that the pastor is doing them no good because he refuses to give them a formula. This is another evidence of their hopelessness in their own eyes. Such self-condemnatory patterns of relatedness and/or unrelatedness are maintained on a legalistic basis. The counselees present a spiraling set of finer and finer distinctions that " lose " any listener in a maze of detailed depreciations of themselves. Such persons more often than not need immediate psychiatric referral and the supportive help a pastor can give.

A more general clinical note needs to be made here concerning the influence of legalistic preaching upon the development of the kind of anxiety evident in such persons as have been described here. In some incidents of such tension the persons have been recently and quite hypnotically affected by the preaching they have heard. Such preaching often propounds a static kind of transactional salvation based upon treadmill-like meriting of God's favor by continually trying to reproduce the form of spiritual experience the preacher himself may have had in his new birth, or the kind he is still trying to conjure up. Not to have had this particular form of conversion apparently consists of having committed the unpardonable sin, resisted the Spirit, grieved the Spirit, or sinned away the days of grace, or not really having been saved.

The place at which the author most often counseled with persons clutched by legalistic anxiety is in New York City. This melting pot of nations and religions receives permissively anyone who wants to get away from anything. Persistently the author has met individuals and groups of persons who have been reared in highly rigid and strictly legalistically religious homes. They have rebelled against the tightness of the irrationally authoritarian teachings of their parents and home communities and have moved to New York where they can find " freedom." They have actually donned an external type of freedom. But within they carry all the loneliness that being cut off from their ancestral home implies. A harsh, unbending rejection and hyperrespectable religion molded into the golden calf of a small town culture show up in the toll they have taken upon the psychic health of these

" lost sheep of the house of Israel." One person in particular felt so completely afraid of her parents' condemnation and rejection that she had changed her name, her address, her work, and every conceivable connection of identity with them. She was wanderingly searching for some expression of the Christian faith that would " heal her of her fears and reveal to her a God of love." The odyssey of her struggle for such meanings was one continual shocking, hurting, and fearful relationship after another.

On the other hand, a visit to the small town religious group to which her parents regularly repaired might reveal the other side of the kind of religion that clothed her unhealthy parent-child relationships with sanctity. Here one might find rigid churchgoing people who have conformed to conventional codes in every detail until they are walking copies of the code and know not what manner of person they really are. Their lives reveal a drab, empty, bored, meaningless existence. They tend to be devoid of the joy of a spontaneous salvation which quite often bubbles up unexpectedly in the fellowship of sinners in a small Holy Roller church where the whole existence of the members is quite often at stake in the things that happen to " bring them out of darkness into light." T. S. Eliot speaks so vividly of such persons when he says:

> " Those who sit in a house of which the use is forgotten . . .
> And they write innumerable books; being too vain and distracted for silence: seeking every one after his own elevation, and dodging his emptiness."

(T. S. Eliot, *Collected Poems,* pp. 194, 195. Harcourt, Brace and Company, Inc., 1936. Used by permission.)

II. LEGALISTIC ANXIETY AND PASTORAL FAILURE
OF COMMUNICATION

Probably the most generally diffuse way in which legalistic anxiety enters the pastoral relationship is in the barrier of respectability which pastors and their people tend to erect between themselves. Some impatient persons would like to assume that this is entirely because of holier-than-thou attitudes on the part of ministers. Ministers themselves may buy this interpretation and develop buddy-buddy relationships with their people which only remotely resemble the fact that they really are interpreters of the mind and way of God. But even so, this divestiture does not accomplish what it manifestly intends to accomplish because parishioners will nevertheless keep their deeper feelings of shame and discrepancy away from the pastor until he is likely to be the very last to hear of their needs. For instance, the shock which many pastors — especially young ones — receive when they discover that the marriage of a couple with whom they have been exceptionally close personal friends is on the verge of divorce is a case in point. As one minister told the author, it was such a blow to him that he was having to reorganize his whole conception of himself as a minister.

Students who graduate from a theological seminary report back occasionally by writing to their professors about their parish work. One rather often-repeated refrain is that the student had very little opportunity for dealing with the more serious problems of his people during the first year he was their pastor. But, after having been there a while, they say, " all these troubles began to come out! " The legalistic expectations which the anxious parishioners assume that the pastor holds for them have been relaxed; they have ceased to treat him as a guest, and have begun to reveal their real selves to him.

This discussion of legalistic anxiety opens the way to a brief study of some of the unique dynamics of the role and function of the pastor and religious worker as a counselor. The socially acceptable deception at work in such relationships is indicative of the cultural walls of partition which separate people from each other in the day-by-day course of their existence. Their petty legalisms have a contrary effect: they protect them from the risks of relating themselves to other people. At the same time, they afflict them with the separation and loneliness that can be supplied only through fellowship with people. The pastoral counselor must go through a maze of vestibules, parlors, ante-

rooms, and waiting rooms before reaching the communion that
really takes place between people in modern society. The façades
of legalistic religion carry with them their own burden of anxiety
lest they prove all too fragile and not nearly so safe as the ones
who trust in façades. The necessity of breaking through these
façades creates the anxiety of those who await real communion
of their real selves as well as anxiety of those who stand at the
door, knock, gain entrance, and establish fellowship with those
who have been so long within themselves that they hardly know
that there is such a thing as communication.

Nevertheless, the stereotypes which insulate pastor and people
from each other muffle, distort, and even annihilate the communion both genuinely need. The processes of personal counseling, therefore, are really experiences of self-revelation in which
counselor and counselee gradually break through these stereotypes and discover who each really is. The anxiety of legalistic
rejection is gradually relieved. This calls for a rigorous adjustment of " who the person thinks the pastor is " to correspond
with his discovery in personal encounter of " who the pastor
really is." The pastor's own struggle with himself lies in his
anxiety to appear other than he really is. This is the pastor's own
stereotype and legalistic anxiety at work within him. This selfhood of the pastor may be called the self " whom he fears himself to be."

On the other hand, the counselee is attempting to communicate his real self. He tests the environment to see if he is accepted
as his " conventional self," or " the self he thinks he is." He fur-
tively begins to reveal the self " whom he fears himself to be."
The experience of clarification and redirection comes in his discovery of the self that he really is, apart from his fantasies of
perfection and his fears of his imperfections. In this sense, the
process of counseling is the overcoming of legalistic anxiety
through the grace of God in a specific human relationship. It
is faith working through love.

Obviously no sharp difference has been drawn here between
counselor and counselee as would make more comfortable some

counselors who have a sort of psychological sinless perfection in their search for a fictitious *total* absence of immaturity. The reasons for identifying the same processes in the counselor as are operative in the counselee are twofold: first, the pastoral counselor usually deals with persons who are not grossly pathological; and, secondly, the legalistic contexts in which modern psychotherapists work are gradually converting a religious legalism into a psychological legalism. This psychological legalism has much shallower roots and hopes are dimmer for a continual softening up of its callousness than is true in the case of religious legalism.

Essentially, however, counseling within the context of the Christian faith is a *reciprocal* pilgrimage between counselor and counselee in the experience of *gracious acceptance* whereby both counselor and counselee accept and affirm each other's basic humanity under God. Much is said about the counselor's acceptance of the counselee. Counselors have just begun to appropriate the companion truth that a part of counseling is the "undeification" of themselves by the counselee and the counselee's acceptance of them as human beings also. If a counselee can do this with his pastor without breaking communication with him, he has grown immeasurably. Whitman sets a poetic description of what goes on in the pilgrimage of pastoral counseling when he says:

" Out from behind this bending rough-cut mask,
   These lights and shades, this drama of the whole,
   This common curtain of the face, contained in me for me, in you
     for you, in each for each.

" (Tragedies, sorrows, laughters, teachers — O Heaven!
   The passionate teeming play this curtain hides!)
   Pausing, inclining, bowing my head, you specially I greet,
   To draw and clinch your soul for once inseparably with mine . . .
   Then travel on, travel on. . . ."

(Walt Whitman, *Leaves of Grass,* pp. 301, 302. Modern Library, Inc., 1944.)

The counselee and the counselor are much more alike than they are different: they both are incurably human, suffering the basically human anxieties of economic survival, the shortness of life, and the continual need for the decisive action of the spirit called faith working through love. This realization is their common ground of acceptance and communication. From here they move to the particular ways in which the counselee has lost his way in the search for the meaning of life and the ways whereby he can find his sense of direction afresh through comparing road maps with the pastoral counselor acting as a sort of " Mr. Interpreter."

The anxiety of legalism, however, prevents them from establishing such an understanding. The community, through its conformity and respectability demands, its legalistic structures, and its wholesaling of stereotypes, purposely excommunicates certain people.

III. Psychotherapeutic Concepts of Compulsive Anxiety

Contemporary psychotherapists have been quick to describe the anxiety of legalism, the inordinate need for the safety of a fixed structure of things. Usually they describe this with such terms as compulsiveness and rigidity. Freud underlined the neurotic elements in religious rituals that had lost their meaning but still were retained and practiced for their anxiety-allaying power. Before him, Friedrich Nietzsche spoke of the death-dealing power of " the preachers of death." He called them the " terrible ones who carry about in themselves the beasts of prey, and have no choice except lusts or self-laceration. And even their lusts are self-laceration." (Friedrich Nietzsche, *Thus Spake Zarathustra,* edited by Manuel Komroff, p. 42. Tudor Publishing Company, 1934.) But Freud, following a less generalized approach, perceived religion among his neurotic patients to be an authoritarian structure built into the character formations of the individual before he arrived at adulthood. External religious authority protected him from his own inner desires to destroy earthly authorities by projecting a benevolent pattern of these parent figures on the cosmic scheme of belief in God. Freud reduced religious practices to the obsessive rituals in neurotic patients, with the exception that they had group sanction whereas the patients who came to him had "private rituals" the meaning of which was ever hidden from them. (Sigmund Freud, "Obsessive Acts and Religious Practices," *Collected Papers,* Vol. II, pp. 25-35. Hogarth Press, 1907.)

In his article on "Civilized Sexual Morality and Modern Nervousness" (*ibid.,* pp. 76-99), he laid the blame for many sexual disorders upon the artificial demands of the religious codes of his day. The clinician notes these harsh religious taboos as they are laid on heterosexual behavior by some legalistically inclined parents and their churches. Such strictures tend to appear later in the child as a preference for homosexual patterns of sexual behavior. Some research needs to be done on this and also upon the kind of religious upbringing a group of alcoholics may have had. One gets a bit uneasy when he sees the repeated instances of alcoholics who have had the finest Christian parents a boy could have wanted. Yet, clinical study of religion at the family level reveals that religion has often been used to maintain a law laid down by the parents who have unexamined and distorted motives for ruling the alcoholic by subtle means.

The psychoanalytic doctrine of the superego may be closely identified with the more compulsive elements of what the apostle Paul spoke of as bondage of the law. As Alexander says: "In the course of time . . . prohibitions and commands of the educational process become transformed into internal laws. . . . This code which has become relegated to the unconscious is identical with the totemistic code of primitive peoples." (William Healy, Augusta F. Bronner, and Anna Mae Bowers, *The Structure and Meaning of Psychoanalysis,* p. 47. Alfred A. Knopf, Inc., 1938.) Referring to the larger religious context of the superego development, Freud says that "it stands as the representative of the most important events in the development of both the individual and the race" (*ibid.,* p. 48). Ernest Jones (Ernest Jones, *What*

Is Psychoanalysis? p. 30; International Universities Press, Inc., 1948.) refers to the superego as the source of irrational guilt, which apparently was built up in terms of what Kelman calls "irrational authorities" in the personal pilgrimage of the individual, i.e., authorities whom the helpless child would feign obey rather than lose their so-called love. Such love would better be called by its right name, fear. (Harold Kelman, "Rational and Irrational Authority: A Holistic Viewpoint," *The American Journal of Psychoanaylsis,* Vol. XII, No. 1, 1952, p. 57.)

At this point, the objective of Christian experience at its best, as well as the objective of psychotherapy at its best, is to "lighten this burden of irrational guilt," i.e., *the deliverance from a body of death.* Whereas these two disciplines appeal to a different source of deliverance and sometimes offer a widely variant interpretation of the meaning of the deliverance once it has been accomplished, they nevertheless agree at two points: (1) the blind, fear-ridden nature of the bondage of legalism, (2) the opposing power of tender love in casting out the fear.

The superego operates, according to psychoanalytic doctrine, on the power of repression, the unconscious process whereby anxiety-creating thoughts and impulses are kept from the ken of consciousness and personal insight. The objective of psychotherapy is to break the power of repression, to make the unconscious conscious and to release the inner strength of the individual for courageous and productive living. Particularly do the psychoanalysts emphasize the release of the love energies for productive interpersonal relationships with people at all levels. They call for a kind of freedom from the compulsive, irrational law which has been built into the character, as will be seen shortly, in the light of what we have already discerned about the teachings of the apostle Paul to the legalistic Jews.

In somewhat the same manner, psychoanalytic concepts have been taken three ways: (1) Some "self-expressionists" in our day, and some of the analysts themselves such as Wilhelm Reich, have taken psychoanalytic teaching as an occasion to the flesh, assuming that *any* kind of self-control is necessarily bad. They feel that sexual and hostile impulses are self-regulatory. Quite often in counseling, pastors meet sophisticated persons who feel that they will make neurotics of their children if they interpret the limits of life to them in any way. These expressionists as adults tend to operate on the principle of indiscriminately and irresponsibly saying and doing what they *feel* like doing regardless of the feelings of others. (2) On the other hand, persons may be met who reject *in toto* the insights of psychotherapists because they penetrate their own defensive structures, threaten the conventional safety values on their own inner strivings, and call for a kind of courage and self-insight they are not prepared to accept. (3) But in a third group, appear persons like John Baillie, who said that psychotherapeutic insights had helped him in his confession of sin! Any attempt to make a one-to-one correlation between psychotherapeutic doctrine and Christian doctrine would reek with philosophical stupidity. However, popular public reaction to the teaching of the psychotherapists has been much like popular misinterpretations of the Christian gospel as it was preached by the apostle Paul. Likewise, many psychotherapists have a more courageous story to tell of their persecutions for their beliefs than have many contemporary Christian preachers!

IV. Toward a Biblical Theology of the Anxiety of Legalism

Both Jewish and Christian writers of the Old and New Testament, respectively, reflect anxiety as to the place of a legal code in their relationship to God and to their religious community. Apparently, a covenant code, or rules for living the religious life, has always served at least three functions in a spiritual fellowship to provide a threefold kind of security for members of the religious group. First, the covenant code has provided a basis for identity, a way of distinction, a pattern of group " selfhood " for the religious commonwealth. Secondly, it has enabled the group to popularize its way of life into a mass religion that is more easily understood, even at the expense of its inner profundities that reach beyond the symbolism of the rituals, social customs, and taboos of the legal code. And, finally, the covenant code helps to resolve the anxiety of religious people over the spiritual destinies of their growing children. Parents satisfy their desire for religious fellowship with their children by developing a religious literature with which to transmit their spiritual tradition from one generation to the next. This literature easily becomes a lawbook for a legalistic spirit to thrive upon. But the most positive use of such writings is evident in Deuteronomy:

" And these words which I command you this day shall be upon your heart; and you shall teach them diligently to your children, and shall talk of them when you sit in your house, and when you walk by the way, and when you lie down, and when you rise. . . . And you shall write them on the doorposts of your house and on your gates." (Deut. 6:6–9.)

However, these three self-maintaining and self-perpetuating motives of a religious group have historically tended to distort distinctly personal lives of individuals, as well as the character of religion itself. The " law " itself can become a substitute for personal encounter with God; it can be the basis for self-righteous defensiveness and avoidance of repentance; it has actually been used as a means for holding it over persons whom the group fears and therefore despises. The tendency to idolatry of the " fathers " of the law also issues in a subtle kind of irreligion in the name of religion itself. This becomes " the bondage of the law," and the wretchedness wrought by this bondage is exactly what is meant by " the anxiety of the law " or legalistic anxiety. Some new apprehension of a less binding kind of security for the spirit is called for; some higher revelation that fulfills but does not destroy the law is certainly indicated for the relief of this kind of anxiety.

The problem of legalistic anxiety and the therapeutic release of Christians from its bondage is a large part of the operational intention of Christian experience as portrayed in the ministry and teachings of Jesus and Paul. In both their teachings freedom in Christ broke the power of sin and the law. If a person had been reared as a son of this or that tribe to depend upon the certainties of the law to relieve him of anxiety, this spiritual freedom set up a conflict within him that amounted to the "anxiety of the law." Paul describes this compulsive need to return to the law and at the same time his struggle to be freed of the law in his classical statement of the character of compulsive or legalistic anxiety in Rom. 7:8: "Sin, finding opportunity in the commandment, wrought in me all kinds of covetousness." As if to say that his very religion itself, i.e., the religion of his fathers, was a source of sin, making him do the wrong that he knew he did not want to do and leave things right undone that he wanted very much to do. In essence he is saying in this passage that sin can so grasp a person that so-called "will power" does not affect its course:

> "So I find it to be a law that when I want to do right, evil lies close at hand. For I delight in the law of God, in my inmost self, but I see in my members another law at war with the law of my mind and making me captive to the law of sin which dwells in my members. Wretched man that I am! Who will deliver me from this body of death?" (Rom. 7:21-24.)

One possible interpretation of this passage is that Paul is describing the wretchedness caused by the continued binding influence of the legalism of the Jews in which he had been reared. He felt the tug of the inbred laws of generations of Judaism. This made him a captive of sin. In fact, in Rom. 7:13 he says that "sin, working death in me through what is good, in order that sin might be shown to be sin, and through the commandment might become sinful beyond measure." Could it be that "this body of death" was the combined inertia of the historically inbred anxieties from generations of the building of "the law" into the structure of his conscience?

Sören Kierkegaard gives a brilliant description of the conflictual nature of this anxiety of legalism. His comment might be taken as a comment on the seventh chapter of Romans. He says:

> "First, a man sins from frailty and weakness; and then — yes, perhaps he learns to flee to God and be helped by faith which saves from all sin; . . . then he despairs over his weakness and becomes either

a Pharisee who in despair manages to attain a certain legal righteousness, or he despairs and plunges into sin." (Sören Kierkegaard, *The Sickness Unto Death*, p. 131.)

Another point of vantage in approaching Paul's " conflict and the law " passage is to say that the apostle was so completely sympathetic with his readers who themselves had this problem that he was identifying their plight with that through which he himself had already come. He certainly reflects in a much more direct way in other places the concern that he had for them, if this is an accurate interpretation. In Rom., ch. 6, he speaks directly to those who have taken the gospel of grace as an occasion to the flesh and chosen to sin all the more in order " that grace may abound." This was one way of handling the anxiety of an inbred legalism: to become antinomians, i.e., those who threw obedience to any law to the wind and " did what came naturally." They were the equivalent of the modern self-expressionists who, after having been cooped up by strictly religious parents, become compulsively aggressive and sensual in every way. To say that they are free is to overlook the fact that they are bound by their rebellion.

Conversely, the apostle spoke directly also to the Galatians who had retreated from the courageous stand of their new-found freedom in Christ to the safe confines of a Judaistic form of Christian faith. They begin to teach that the only persons qualified for entrance into the Christian community were those who adhered to the law:

"Formerly, when you did not know God, you were in bondage to beings that by nature are no gods; but now that you have come to know God, or rather to be known by God, how can you turn back again to the weak and beggarly elemental spirits, whose slaves you want to be once more? . . . For freedom Christ has set us free; stand fast therefore, and do not submit again to a yoke of slavery. Now I, Paul, say to you that if you receive circumcision, Christ will be of no advantage to you." (Gal. 4:8,9; 5:1,2.)

Paul's preaching of the freedom of the gospel, therefore, created three kinds of anxiety reactions among his hearers: (1) the

reaction of unbridled self-expression and irresponsibility after
having been "liberated" by the gospel; (2) the reaction of trans-
ferring the old legalism of Judaism to the Christian faith, or, to
use the parable of Jesus, putting the new wine in old wineskins;
(3) the mixed reaction of first an unbridled self-expression and
then a reaction of extreme legalism. All three of these reactions
reflect a high degree of compulsive and involuntary attitudes and
actions. These were security operations of anxious people who
had long come to depend upon the safe legalisms of the external
authoritarianism of the older religion of Judaism. When they
sought to lay aside the crutches of these external supports they
became compulsively anxious. Such anxiety is accurately called
legalistic anxiety.

Later within the Christian community itself, an adulation of
the legalistic influences of Judaism, *anxiety over structure and
form* (which is another way of describing legalistic anxiety), appeared. Persons who spontaneously experienced personal religious
rebirths sought to recapture repeatedly the luminous radiance of
the experience that had been theirs. Spiritual children that they
were, they wanted to feel the thrill of it again. They became ec-
static Christians who "legalized" a certain form of religious
experience — i.e., prophecy, healing, speaking of tongues, etc.
They were charismatic Christians insisting upon the pre-eminence of their particular gift and losing communication with
people of different gifts. They became intolerant extremists who
tried to enforce this "gift" upon others. In doing so they developed a party spirit which threatened the fellowship of the
churches to which Paul ministered. Other Christians escaped the
anxiety of Christian freedom itself by displacing some of their
legalistic anxiety into new legalistic "molds" (to use Tertul-
lian's term). They concerned themselves with the externalism
of ritualistic forms, and invested ritual forms with such meaning that these became forms of legalistic demand for Christians. These in turn were sytematized into the patterns of creed
and ecclesiastical behavior which later became known as the
forensic structure of the Catholic Church.

The Protestant Reformation represents a burst-through of the forms of Christianity with the reaffirmation of the creativity of the Christian freedom. Nevertheless, the vital emphasis upon justification by faith and freedom from the law of Catholicism met with many of the excesses which Paul also confronted. As Richard Baxter, a Protestant pastor, once said, one (and only one) reason why Protestants revolted against the idea of the confessional was to avoid the necessity of confessing their sins at all.

The process of shifting old security operations in the management of anxiety to new forms of Protestant legalism, however, was not long in getting under way. Overstated, bizarre, and harsh use of the Bible became a substitute for older forms of law-security safety valves in a free community. (This point is developed in the author's book *The Bible in Pastoral Care.* The Westminster Press, 1953.) Likewise, Protestant legalism took up many of the preoccupations of the Early Church which protected the early Christians from the responsibilities of their freedom in Christ. Protestants have divided, subdivided, and fallen into all sorts of failures of communication over forms of Christian ritual, interpretations of Christian literature, and forms of Church government. These issues cannot be reduced to a mere matter of handling anxiety; to do so would be "psychologism" at its worst. Great principles have been hammered out on the anvil of these concerns. Nevertheless, compulsive anxiety is *one* factor at work in these heated discussions.

The tension is usually drawn between two groups: in the first group are those persons who have need for a close, legal, and semantically familiar definition of religion that will provide them with a maximum of safety and subject them to a minimum of fear. In the second group are those persons who have a need to rebel against such definitions in order to assert their independence. Curiously enough, both groups are often motivated by the same kind of security operations against anxiety working under different semantic descriptions and different signal reactions of theological jargon. Somewhere apart from either group is a less

compulsive, less rigid, more mellowed group of persons who are
not taken in by the more demonic elements in either of the other
two groups. They are usually called " sons of God " in the mind
of Christ, for they are the peacemakers. They have a way of seeing
the situation steady and seeing it whole, as did Gamaliel on an
auspicious occasion.

The bold contrasts of the story of the two sons in Jesus' parable
of the Prodigal and the Elder Brother reveal the difference between the adventurous self-abandon and rich love of the father
for the younger son and the self-centered legalism of the elder
son. These characters in the parable reflect the difference between
a religion of secure personal redemptiveness in dealing with a
sinner as over against the religion of managed perfection, self-
righteousness, and competitive comparison which ostracizes him.
These two approaches, furthermore, epitomize the difference
between the religion of joy and spontaneous fellowship and the
religion of bored bitterness and excluding withdrawal. Such a
contrasting description of the religious relatedness of God to the
" lost sheep of the house of Israel " — the publicans and sinners —
and that of those *safe* in the fold, i.e., the Pharisees, was drawn by
Jesus himself. The whole message of Jesus was addressed to alienated, excommunicated, and disassociated conditions within the
commonwealth of the spiritual community. He felt keenly the
wideness of the fixed gulf between the outcasts and those whose
legalistic safety measures had excommunicated them. He affirmed
the power of his love to establish community with them again,
without at the same time excusing them from the fixed fact of
their sinfulness. He manifested that perfect love which would
cast out their fear of punishment whereby law would be overcome by grace.

However, the contemporaries of Jesus considered him as an
offender, a winebibber, and a glutton in points respecting the law.
They frowned upon his concern for those who had been excommunicated by the law. In the context of this disapproval Jesus
told the stories of the Lost Sheep, the Lost Coin, and the Lost
Brother. Whereas the prodigal son was dead to the law, the elder

brother was dead in the law. And, for having preached this gospel of redemption, Jesus was crucified according to the law.

The apostle Paul related the redemptive death of Christ to the
Christian's release from the binding anxiety of the law. Here
again the Christian experience of the cross is a way of " life
through death " to the stifling effects of the law. As the apostle
Paul says:

" You have died to the law through the body of Christ, so that you
may belong to another, to him who has been raised from the dead in
order that we may bear fruit for God. . . . But now we are discharged from the law, dead to that which held us captive, so that
we serve not under the old written code but in the new life of the
Spirit." (Rom. 7:4,6.)

THE ANXIETY REACTIONS OF
THE MORALLY INDIFFERENT

I. CALLOUSNESS: A WAY OF LIFE

The varieties of anxiety that have been set forth in the preceding chapters represent considerable amounts of sensitivity in the anxious person. He is aware of a painful uneasiness of mind. He is not indifferent to his situation. He usually seeks help for his difficulty because of his self-concern if for no other reason.

The experienced pastor, however, knows that his community has a considerable number of people who act out rather than feel their anxiety. They have little awareness of any painful uneasiness of mind at all. They do not lie awake nights and worry over their sins, nor do they sit in preoccupation wondering if they have done wrong. They do not consciously seem to care (which is a type of anxiety) that there be such a thing as the law, the rules of the game, or responsibility to others. They rarely go to anyone for help except when they are about to be caught by one authority person or another, or when they are looking for someone whom they can " use " for their own purposes. They are the indifferent ones. Whatever anxiety their behavior represents may be called " the anxiety reactions of the morally indifferent."

The pastor encounters such persons indirectly more often than not. They themselves do not come to him for counseling help ordinarily. Their relatives and friends are concerned about the amount of trouble they can cause and come to the pastor for help. Their relatives' concern is quite often of an overprotective nature that sedulously relieves the person of the privilege of learning from his or her own experience. This concern is partly motivated by the family's desire to protect themselves from public embarrassment by their relatives, partly by emotional needs to keep the black sheep dependent upon their directions, and partly by an ever-fleeing hope that *they* will be able to save their loved one.

For instance, the two sisters of a forty-one-year-old woman sought personal guidance in what to do about their sister. She had been a chronic alcoholic for fifteen years, had been arrested on prostitution charges twenty-three times, and had been married and divorced three times. The pastor spent over an hour simply getting the story of the number of persons to whom the sisters had been for help on behalf of their sister, but was not able to discover a single situation in which the offending person had ever sought help except on occasions when she needed money or to be bailed out of jail. As one doctor described a patient of his who was similar to this person, " She needs to be in the kind of institution which does not yet exist, and which has not yet been even thought of." Such persons know the difference between right and wrong, but the difference does not bother them. They handle whatever anxiety they have by narcotizing it. Their behavior has a certain smooth, mechanical character which seems to operate quite apart from any anxiety of self-control.

These persons are not always to be found among the religious portions of the population. Occasionally they are to be found in religious garb also. Sinclair Lewis, to the great discomfort of the Protestant clergy, caricatured the ministry by describing this kind of person in *Elmer Gantry*. The pampering of ministers, their tendency to make things sacred commonplace, and their lack of specific authority to outline their duties and lay down expectations of them make them susceptible to becoming presumptuous upon the very laws of the God they proclaim. They feel too often that they can get bread without working, and they can gain status in a community without observing the plain rules of fair play, and that they will be able to defy any given set of rules without penalty but always as the exception to the rule. But even with these tempting opportunities, only a few such persons actually get into the active ministry. When they do get beyond the screening procedures of the Christian fellowship, they can create an indeterminate amount of havoc in a given church fellowship, filling the newspapers with their bizarre escapades.

Church fellowship and theological education communities present mixed feelings when the necessity for dealing with such gross indifference to moral values appears in their group. Legalistic, sentimental, psychotherapeutic, and exposé techniques of treatment all come to the fore in discussions of what to do about such individuals.

Pastors also encounter similar confusion in their flock when they have to deal with scandals created by a homosexual church member, by church members who chronically steal from others, etc. These persons not only do these things, but also teach others to do them. A doctor might say of some types of persons with this difficulty that therapy has very little to offer them. They often, but not always by any means, seem very comfortable about their problem and do not seem alarmed about the reality difficulties it presents them. They are perfectly willing to undergo treatment if it means they can hold their job, but psychiatrists may tell the pastor that they feel pretty hopeless about doing much for them in as much as they have so little anxiety. As one doctor described such a patient, he said, " He sits there comfortably in his chair and we talk quietly about his trouble as if it were an extraneous piece of protoplasm which he expects me to remove by surgery! "

II. Toward an Understanding of the Dynamics of the Morally Indifferent

Some sort of working hypothesis as to the dynamics of the moral indifference of the persons described here is prerequisite to dealing with such persons. If one followed the assumptions of the psychiatrists just mentioned, he might conclude that a discussion of these persons is irrelevant to a book on anxiety in Christian experience. They, as far as appearance goes, show neither anxiety nor Christian experience. But such an attitude would be superficial indeed, even though it is the point at which both psychiatry and pastoral practice have tended to stop.

The development of the personality of morally indifferent persons often reflects moral inconsistency in the parental treatment they received. In other situations, moral indulgence is evident. In all instances, the personal histories of such individuals reveal an absence of dependable authority persons with whom they could identify and like whom they could safely become because of their deep admiration for them. The " protoplasm " of the spirit of which the conscience is grown is created and sustained in such relationships. The absence of anxiety reflects the absence of relatedness to trusted persons whose approval genuinely matters to the individual.

The concept of the development of personality set forth by Sören Kierkegaard provokes some insight into the dynamics of the morally indifferent from a developmental point of view. The first stage of the development of a spiritual selfhood, according to Kierkegaard, is the *aesthetic* stage. In this stage, a person, regardless of his chronological age is like unto a Don Juan who is dominated by infinite passion for all women and never bothered by personal responsibility to any one. A person in this stage is absorbed only in the immediate, and has no concern for past or future. His desires in the immediacy of the present moment call for infinite satisfaction with no eye to the consequences of such fulfillment. He does not reflect upon his desires, because to do so would be to knock the edge of immediacy from them. He is characterized by the young person also, says Kierkegaard. As Swenson interprets this personality,

" He has an intelligence which has compassed the world in reflection, but he lacks the experience of a decisive personal commitment to anything in life. . . . He is a possibility who has so far postponed a decisive action." (David Swenson, *Something About Kierkegaard*, pp. 169, 170. Augsburg Publishing House, 1945.)

This person, according to Kierkegaard, is morally dead, and this is evident the moment he opens his mouth. He cannot stand the tension of an ethical dilemma and would rather talk about something else, because he is like unto a child unto whom everything seems impossible and who defers the day of ethical choice. When confronted with such tension, he says with Scarlet O'Hara, " I won't think about that today; I will think about that tomorrow." But tomorrow never comes, because he lives in the present. Such a person is typified in the young wife who, when caught in a clandestine love affair with another man, said: " I just can't choose between them. I love them both and want them both. I have always had everything I wanted and now at the age of twenty-five I can't seem to make any decisions about things." She was confronting divorce.

Jesus sensed this kind of searing of conscience as one of the inner conditions of which divorce was an outward result. He said for the hardness of the hearts of men and women, Moses had granted them the writs of divorcement. His own prophetic actions and teachings throw the light of his ethical concern on the situation of all morally indifferent persons.

In Jesus' teachings an ethical realism serves as a dark background for the bright light of his love, showing it up in its completeness. For him to call darkness light, bitter sweet, and bad good would have been to misrepresent reality to his followers and to have done an unloving thing to those who thrashed about in the anxiety of their self-deification. Therefore he spoke plainly to those who shut up the Kingdom of Heaven against men, neither entering themselves nor allowing those who would enter to go in. He roundly rebuked those who had become insensitive to the weightier matters of the law through religious professionalism. He spoke of eternal punishment for those who had lost the power to sense the needs of the stranger, the hungry, the thirsty, and the naked, and those in bondage, or to feel the brunt of oppression.

Furthermore, Jesus spoke of persons who " seeing do not see, and hearing do not hear." The context of this moral insensitivity helps one to understand Jesus' quotation from Isa. 6:9,10 in Matt. 13:14,15:

" ' You shall indeed hear but never understand,
    and you shall indeed see but never perceive.
For this people's heart has grown dull,
    and their ears are heavy of hearing,
    and their eyes have closed,
lest they should perceive with their eyes,
    and hear with their ears,
and understand with their heart,
    and turn for me to heal them.' "

This is a passive kind of indifference and moral lassitude amounting to spiritual obtuseness. The active and aggressive kind of resistance to repentance and change of character is apparent in the teaching of Jesus about the blasphemy against the Holy Spirit:

" But whoever blasphemes against the Holy Spirit never has forgiveness, but is guilty of an eternal sin." (Mark 3:29.)

The callousness to reconciliation, the refusal to confront and to become aware of the anxiety of sin and guilt, finitude and human frailty, and the need for creative change and a rebirth of the self — these were perceived to be active opposition to the Holy Spirit.

The teachings of the apostle Paul serve to deepen the understanding of the dynamics of the morally indifferent and their strange, repressed anxiety. Paul describes such a condition in Eph. 4:18,19:

" They are darkened in their understanding, alienated from the life of God because of the ignorance that is in them, due to their hardness of heart; they have become callous and have given themselves up to licentiousness, greedy to practice every kind of uncleanness."

Here Paul is describing the person who has lost the capacity to feel anxiety. His only anxiety is over the return of sensitivity to ethical concerns and interpersonal values. Paul registers real pessimism here about the person whose sense of moral responsibility and social feeling has become calloused, hardened over, and whose sources of tender spiritual insight have been desensitized to the point of apathy. The term for " having become callous " is translated in older translations as " being past feeling." It comes from a word which in other connections means " to cease to feel pain " and from which we also transliterate the root verb to get our word " analgesic," a kind of pain-killing preparation for rubbing sore muscles.

A figure of speech that helps to clarify further this kind of anxiety is " anesthetized " anxiety, similar to the condition of the surgical patient who has received pain-killing drugs to narcotize his sensitivity to suffering. He lives, therefore, with a braced awareness that the pain may return. This is his anxiety. Figuratively, therefore, the morally insensitive person is much like this: he lives by constantly bracing himself against the sense of moral pain. Paul speaks again of this kind of handling of anxiety in the Letter to the Romans. He speaks of idolaters who have become " futile in their thinking and their senseless minds were darkened " (Rom. 1:21). In the older translations of later verses in this context, reference is made to a " reprobate mind."

Kierkegaard's idea of the infinite and omnipotent nature of the desires of such a person stands out in Paul's reference to their greediness and insatiable desires. The idea is originally that of always wanting more and more. Such lack of acceptance of limitations, and avoidance of discipline repudiates the claims of others to be considered as anything other than as means toward the satisfaction of desire. Actually it becomes a hedonistic idolatry of desire, and usually the many desires of an individual war for ascendancy in this self-worship. As Paul says, they have " exchanged the truth about God for a lie and worshiped and served the creature rather than the Creator " (Rom. 1:25).

A further analysis of the dynamics of the morally indifferent appears, interestingly enough, in the concept of moral indifference in relation to repression enunciated by O. Hobart Mowrer, a contemporary research psychotherapist, in his book *Learning Theory and Personality Dynamics*. He also makes note of the overindulgence of children and adults by authority persons such as parents and teachers because of their fear that an honest interpretation of the limitations of reality living would make neurotics of their charges. He says that moral indifference is the result of such overindulgence and misrepresentation of the ethical structure of human relationships. He reinterprets the Freudian concept of repression by saying that Freud had a misleadingly limited understanding of his own concept of repression. Freud taught that anxiety is a vague and objectless apprehension that impulses of lust and hostility would "erupt back into consciousness." Mowrer criticizes and takes issue with him over reducing anxiety to apprehension over this kind of eruption. To the contrary, he says that repression can move also in the direction of inhibiting the moral strivings of the individual, and anxiety can be just as intense, causing the person to act out his lustful and aggressive impulses without control. He says:

"Many sources of present evidence indicate that most — perhaps all — neurotic human beings suffer, not because they are unduly inhibited as regards their biological drives, because they have disavowed and repudiated their own moral strivings. Anxiety comes, not from repressed sexuality or pent-up hatred, but from a denial and defiance of the forces of conscience." (O. Hobart Mowrer, *Learning Theory and Personality Dynamics,* p. 568. Ronald Press, 1950.)

He goes on to point out that modern man is becoming increasingly *afraid of his anxieties.* He conceives of personality disorders as arising from moral rather than biological frustrations, and challenges his fellow psychotherapists to come to grips with "the riddle of the unhinged soul," which he conceives to be primarily due to the loss of ethical concern and a desensitization to the inherent validity of the Ten Commandments even apart from their authorship. He speaks of the neurotic strategies the basic mechanisms of which are all the same: "devices for neutralizing conscience."

Professor Mowrer has moved into a more realistic direction for the solution of many psychotherapeutic problems upon which Freudian hypotheses have been long on theory and short on therapy. However, one should qualify the impression that Mowrer leaves that lustful and hostile repressions are not also sources of real anxiety reactions. He almost falls into an "either-or sand-trap" at this point. Not to make this qualification would be to

overlook the express statement of Freud himself when he said
that

"conflict is not resolved by helping one side (of the personality conflict between desires and prohibitions) to win the victory over the
other. . . . If we were to make victory possible merely to the sensual
side instead, the disregarded forces repressing sexuality would have
to indemnify themselves by symptoms. . . . People who can be so
easily influenced by a physician would have found their own way to
that solution without this influence." (Sigmund Freud, *A General
Introduction to Psychoanalysis,* pp. 375, 376. Garden City Publishing
Company, Inc., 1943.)

III. The Responses of the Christian Fellowship
to the Morally Indifferent

A clear word needs to be said to the effect that the term "moral
indifference" as it is used here does not necessarily refer to the
person who is a good moral man but never goes to church.
Church attendance is important but is not the point of focus in
this discussion. One may rightly ask for some more specific descriptions of the way in which morally indifferent persons react
within the Christian fellowship. Such descriptions will help clarify the various responses that can be made to the needs of such
persons. Two typical patterns of behavior tend to occur quite
often. In both patterns a kind of hardness of heart and head
appear in the interpersonal unrelatedness of the individual giving the trouble.

For instance, in the first place, a given individual may con-
sistently interpret any tenderness on the part of others as weakness, stupidity, and a signal for his own exploitation. He exploits
the kindness he meets in others to the fullest and uses the kind
person until he no longer needs him. Then, if the person has not
already lost patience with him, blown his top, and broken his
relationship to him, the apathetic exploiter ditches him and no
longer has any use for him. He plays his victims for suckers and
capitalizes on their permissiveness to the point of goading them
to reject him. Some pastors follow this course of action with

many problem persons in their community. They, by reason of their need to be a do-gooder as well as their traditional role as a kind person, are often taken in by this exploitatively insensitive individual. A pastoral counselor is usually afraid of his own hostilities toward the person and tends to compensate for these feelings by appeasement policies. The person senses, however, the depths of the rejection and reacts to it in kind, becoming all the more destructive as he acts out his anxiety.

In a second instance, the hardness of heart spoken of here may appear in another form. The person may be basically threatened by tenderness. He interprets it as a sign of guilt on the part of the pastoral counselor for some real or supposed wrong he feels that the pastor is reputed to have done him. This is what the psychiatrists would call a persecutory reaction. One never forgets the jolt that he receives when he first learns that some people are frightened by closeness and affection, threatened by tenderness and concern. They may even be panicked into disruptive behavior by it. Occasionally such a persecuted personality is threatened by tenderness on the part of his pastor and other friends. He becomes irreconcilably critical of those who have been closest, most helpful, and tender toward him. He develops a " sandy spot of reality " as a basis for his complaints and pushes his hostility vengefully, harshly, uncompromisingly, and to the hurt of all who get in his way. Nothing persons can do will set their relationship straight with him, and any attempt at clarification is distorted and becomes new timber for the feeling that all are against him.

A rather commonplace (but all the more difficult for that reason) example of this appears in the following pastoral situation:

I first met Bill Smith four years ago when I became pastor of the church of which he is a member. At that time he was nearly thirteen and, with rare exceptions, was always at church with his mother; however, the father or older brother never attended. During the intervening years I have pieced together the following information about the boy and his family: Bill is the youngest of four children, the two oldest ones being married. His only brother, age twenty-five and single, is the tough, hard-working son who has stayed home to

help care for their two-hundred-acre farm. The father is quite antag-
onistic to religion, but is a morally sound man. The older son, though
not hostile to religion, has followed in his father's example of having
little or nothing to do with church. This son and the father have been
quite close to each other, but the father says Bill is weak, lazy, and
will hardly work. It is reported that the mother told her husband when
Bill was born, " You have raised the other boy and I will raise this
one." Accordingly, she has taken Bill to church with her regularly.

Bill is popular at school, making good grades and taking a leading
role in campus activities. However, he is most at home when with
girls. He himself has effeminate gestures and actions, and on one occasion a girl told me, " We look upon him as being one of the girls."
He hardly associates at all with boys of the church. The fact that he
is the only boy in our young people's choir does not phase him in the
least from regular attendance.

Approximately a year after I became his pastor, Bill made it known
to me in private that he was considering entering the ministry. Later
at a special church program he made a short speech and was highly
complimented by members of the church. Shortly thereafter he made
a public decision to do full-time Christian work. At this time Bill
became most voluminous in his letter writing to me, writing at the
slightest occasion concerning a party, my sermon, a girl, etc. Once he
wrote me that his doctor had told him that he would die as a young
man. Upon his returning to the church, I told him I would like to
talk with him concerning the matter, but he deferred the subject
" until later." He has never mentioned it again.

About this time I became aware of the fact that Bill and I were having considerable difficulty communicating in a face-to-face situation;
he seemed to block, although he was able to express himself very
well by letter. This problem has become increasingly apparent in
the last two years. However, he is quite free in the presence of my
wife, but when I join the group he " clams up."

Bill is known in the church as something of an impetuous boy who
speaks his mind without much apparent forethought. For instance,
on one occasion he decided that he was going to sing a solo in church
the following Sunday. Since he is almost a monotone, I suggested that
he wait until he could practice further on the song. However, the
following week I received a letter from him informing me that I was
wrong and that he was going to sing the next Sunday. Taking this
as an adolescent trait, I let him sing. Then, too, there have been other
instances of this type of behavior. Yet, the adults of the church con-

sider him one of the finest and most promising young men of the church.

Our real problems began one Sunday morning when I forgot and left my Bible on the pulpit. At a special program that night Bill was to read several passages from the Bible, and it appeared to me that he was using my Bible. After the service was over I forgot to see him about it. During the following week I had occasion to write him and put a P.S. on my letter stating I thought I had seen him with the Bible and would appreciate it if he would keep it until I returned. This P.S. provoked a most hostile letter from him in which he asserted that I had accused him of thievery and that he was " very mad." After a three-day cooling-off period, I wrote him stating I could see how my note could have been misunderstood and explained the whole situation, whereupon he wrote back apologizing (as he had done in the singing instance).

However, it was obvious in the ensuing months by the coldness and distance between Bill and myself that the wound had not healed. He now began a series of moves in which he tried to move counter to anything he felt I wanted to do. Prior to his explosion of temper I had asked him to preach some night, to which he had agreed and had already selected a text. The first example of his rebellion was his later refusal to preach on this night. Then he decided he would not be a preacher but rather a minister of education. Again he decided he would not attend a college he and a group of our young people (including myself) had visited but instead would go to another one.

After our revival last year Bill wrote me that the evangelist's and my " inspiring sermons " had made it clear to him that God wanted him to preach. The following Sunday he came in tears rededicating his life. That afternoon I again approached him but, as before, he seemed to block, except for some superficial remarks about his school work, at face-to-face communication.

At present our church is planning a week youth revival in April, and I naturally turned to Bill to serve as youth pastor since he has indicated his plan to become a minister. The day he was approached on the subject he happened to be sick at home. I noted that he became quite nervous when the subject was introduced, and presently one of our young people, Jane, who had gone with my wife and myself, broke in and asked, " Bill, is it true or not what you told me the other day? " He replied in the negative and accepted the offer to be youth pastor. Sensing something was wrong, I asked Jane, while returning, if Bill had had a problem. She indicated that he had but was somewhat reluctant to talk, therefore I did not press the issue.

That night after the services Jane apologized for being somewhat reticent in the afternoon and then told me this story: About two weeks prior to this time Bill had told her he could no longer believe as Methodists did and that he did not bow his head any more when we prayed. He stated that he had become a member of a Catholic church in a town five miles away, and that he attended early Mass plus the services at our church because he feared some recrimination from our people should these things be known.

He further stated that his mother knew of this (which is highly improbable since such information would literally crush her spirit). He also displayed some Catholic medals, and stated that Catholics prayed to Mary because of their unworthiness to approach Christ directly. Jane said he told her he would not accept the youth pastor position if it was offered to him because he was now a Catholic.

I asked Jane how widely these matters were known in the community, and she stated that nearly all the girls in their junior class knew and approximately six girls in our church were aware of this. One girl, a member of the Baptist church, had asked her a few days before whether or not it was true that the stewards of our church were calling a special meeting to "kick Bill out of the church." Therefore, it seems that this matter is becoming common knowledge among the members of the community. Since our church and community is a close-knit, rural situation, this could have great repercussions.

What, then, are some of the responses that a Christian fellowship could make to such situations as these and others like them? The first response to such rebelliousness would be violent hostility, and the pastor and people alike tend to become angry with such a person. In a sense, he is acting out the pattern of rebellion that he has always used in response to rejection. He acts out his anxiety in such a way as to *cause* others who would be kind to him to lose patience with him and reject him. In fact, he is testing the "patience quotient" of all concerned to see how much he can get by with, how far he can go.

A second response possible in this situation is to pamper and overindulge the person. Attempts to look upon him as sick often amount to just this and turn out to be maudling sentimentality rather than realistic understanding. In acting out his anxiety about the authority persons in the situation, the person is also counting quietly on the overindulgence of the sentimental ones. In fact, the pastor may be almost a " mothering influence " in his life.

A third response would be to represent reality to the person. This implies a balance between permitting the person to profit by his own mistakes and avoiding vindictive acts of reprisal toward him. When a person is definitely out of bounds ethically and interpersonally, those whom he has offended do him harm when, out of some sense of timidity or fear of him, they refrain from an honest expression of their sense of injustice. Professor Ross Snyder underlines this ethical structure of interpersonal relationships when he says:

" Part of the experience of love is the justice-giving demand which we experience within us and toward others. ' This is not fair; this is unjust! ' cannot be disregarded if man is to survive in society. For injustice is a violation of man as a human being and of the Holy in the universe." (Ross Snyder, " Religious Living with Three and Four Year Olds," *The Chicago Theological Seminary Register,* Vol. XLIII, No. 1, January, 1953.)

Such violations of human personality should be called to a morally insensitive person's attention in a disciplined and orderly way. The administrative organization of the home, the church, the school, the hospital, or the larger community should be set up in such a decent and orderly way that instances like this can be handled in a similar manner. Whatever aggression is expressed toward an individual should be done as a corporate responsibility of the group as a whole to which the individual is responsible, rather than as the unguided hostility of an individual person, even of the pastor. This deals realistically with the problem of authority in community living. Such authority should be mobilized and expressed in a responsible way. If this is done so as to represent reality vividly and without vindictiveness to the individual, he tends to become more secure for having learned where the bounds of his habitation are. His anxiety reactions are lessened and he becomes more sensitive to the corporate fellowship to which he belongs. Mowrer indicates that this is a part of the dynamic development of healthy personality and implies a wholesome kind of aggressiveness in individual and corporate actions:

" No society can be a going concern unless there is some form of political authority. We sometimes make the mistake of thinking of aggressive behavior as being exclusively antisocial. We must remember that there is also such a thing as *prosocial* aggression, and that it is an essential element in parental discipline and in community control." (*Op. cit.*, p. 569.)

But this talk of the place of aggression in dealing with morally indifferent persons will raise active questions in the minds of pastors who have become conversant with current trends in pastoral counseling. They will ask how this can be harmonized with the more permissive relationship of the typical counseling situation. Two things need to be said here: First, the pastor is not counseling, in the technical sense of the word, in dealing with morally insensitive persons. He is usually involved in some administrative or disciplinary action, which, if he is able to use his authority to create an awareness of the need for counseling, may in a real way be a precounseling situation. Ordinarily the pastor will call for the help of some other counselor to provide the more permissive type of relationship. In the second place, the kind of anxiety reaction here is such that permissiveness may be interpreted as license, as a sign of weakness, and as an opportunity for exploitation of the social position of the pastoral counselor. In other words, in an uncontrolled, intimately involved pastoral situation, the amount of jeopardy to the pastor's total function is great. He may be too socially and emotionally involved in the situation to be the most helpful counselor to such an individual. If he attempts to distort the actual authority in the real social role that he does have in the life of the person, the person senses it as a sort of misrepresentation of the real situation and tends to force the pastor sooner or later to use the authority he does have.

In dealing with morally indifferent persons, the pastor cannot assume the same kind of relationship that he would have with persons who reflect even superficial concern about their life situation. A different problem exists, a different understanding is called for; and a different approach is necessary. In the terms of the psychological realities at hand, the pastor has to re-evaluate his concept of counseling as being a *totally* permissive and unstructured relationship. It actually is not.

Many pastors have raised this question in a different form when they have said: "Modern counselors insist upon a 'nondirective' procedure. This throws us in conflict with our task as prophets who stand up against evil and injustice. How can we reconcile our role as a prophet with our work as a counselor if this is the whole story about counseling? This is not in keeping with the responsibility we bear to the whole church and our obligation to protect the flock of invaders." Furthermore, such pastors will quote innumerable references in the Biblical account where the prophets, Jesus, and the apostles were quite forthright in what they had to say.

In dealing with his people, the Christian pastor has to combine the elements of authoritativeness with the elements of permissive love, even as he functions both as a prophet and as a counselor. In this his people find a dependable and yet free relationship with their minister that leads them to the healing of their crippling anxieties and enables them to take advantage of the power of their basic human anxieties. This is exactly what the Old Testament prophets and the New Testament apostles did. Naturally, they knew their own weakness, and did not presume perfection. Nevertheless, the time came when they felt called upon to speak clearly against hard hearts and to challenge the behavior of the disrupters of the community. Like these prophets, also, the pastor will need to rely upon the cleansing power of prayer at this point more than most others. For here, with inner awareness of his own weaknesses, he knows that he prophesies in part. Pastors can learn from the prophets who went into the temple of worship and purified their lips of sin before they appeared before people or individuals. They conferred with each other for wisdom and spiritual solidarity. Then they spoke in plain words of impeccable courage to the injustices and encumbrances of unreality which they saw about them. They talked to hardened hearts, fattened ears, and blinded eyes in their particular ages of anxiety when their people had become apathetic to each other's needs and to the meaning of their relationship and ultimate destiny in God.

The seeming contradictions raised by these questions draw into focus the fact that the pastoral counselor always works within the context of a specific religious community, namely, the church. What he does, he does not alone. He represents the social reality of the needs of the whole community as well as the inner reality of the overwhelming desires of the individual. Pastoral relationships, like parent-child relationships, therefore combine the tougher realism of social demand with the more tender satisfactions of personal concern for the individual. When one finds these two factors in balanced proportion in a pastor, he usually finds a pastor whose personhood unites courageous strength with secure tenderness. Such a combination of the rod and staff of a true shepherd places a pastor in the tradition of the prophets. The absence of either strength or tenderness tends to create the kind of anxiety reactions that have been discussed here. In a very real way, the Christian community is always at work balancing up these deficiencies in the way in which it deals with the anxieties of the persons to whom it ministers.

The ordering of the Christian community as it challenges and disciplines the morally indifferent usually is set in motion by its leadership, which often turns out to be the pastor. The pastor symbolizes the prophetic tension between the justice-demanding and compassion-expressing character of the community. When he speaks prophetically to an offender within the community, he need not expect to be liked. He should only be concerned that he speaks for God and the Christian fellowship and not for himself. Such a pattern of relatedness on his part puts him on the spot in such a way that he can at least catch a glimpse of the loneliness of the prophets and of Jesus. The cross becomes a reality to him in such instances, because to take up such a role in society is to ask for a deeper participation in the meaning of the cross than one has known before. Therefore, Jesus asks every aspiring disciple if he is able to drink of the cup that he drank and to be baptized with the baptism wherewith he was baptized! Prophecy is more than calling fire down on people who insult the prophet. It is participation in the redemptive seriousness into which Jesus has called the prophet.

As such a prophet encounters the morally insensitive, the reality of the cross itself becomes very apparent in the interpersonal relationship if the challenged one sees it at all. The Holy Spirit sensitizes the indifferent by the combined firmness and affection of the man of God or the people of God. If it were not for the sharp contradictions of the cross, man would have remained impervious to the radical difference between destructive sinfulness and redemptive love. Once such a difference is felt, an anxiety is awakened, and " chords that were broken vibrate once more." Yet even this calls for the creative anxiety of the cross.

CHAPTER

7

THE ANXIETY OF THE CROSS

I. The New Birth of a New Self

All the types of anxiety mentioned thus far are preludes to a deeper and more creative uneasiness of spirit — the anxiety of the cross. Each of these kinds of anxiety calls for a spiritual rebirth, which in actuality is a death, burial, and resurrection to a newer and more secure life through faith. The tyranny of the tangible in economic anxiety is broken by taking up the cross and following the Lord Jesus Christ. The breathless shortness of life is set in the context of eternity by the acceptance of one's finitude as a prerequisite to birth into the realm of the eternal. The death, burial, and resurrection becomes an intimate reality in the resolution of the anxiety of grief. Dying to sin and rising to the new life in God through the forgiveness made available through faith in Christ reveals again the purposiveness of the cross in the resolution of the anxiety of sin. The destructive effects of the law are set at nought by the death to the law through the grace of God. And the morally insensitive and indifferent are brought to an awareness of God and their fellows through the prophetic challenge of the cross.

Yet the cross itself presents the most intense anxiety of all, the tension of an impending birth of a new life. The awesome realization of the possibility of being borne out of the narrow confines of these various kinds of anxiety involves the anxiety of creation itself. The impending necessity of a new life presents what Isaiah calls "sheer terror" in itself. The inner yearning for a new being in Christ is qualitatively described in the despair of the following counselee:

A feeling deep inside where hidden talents lie and wait for freedom, I wander through a lost feeling of loneliness and distress, wondering what to expect as I'm tottering on the edge of despair. A feeling that so fills my soul and being, a feeling that keeps me from enjoying the beauty of the earth and its inhabitants, I wonder why this soul is left on earth to wander alone through its hidden valleys of self-torture, for one soul can torture itself to destruction.

I wait each night for that lost feeling, until its thoughts and weariness embezzle themselves into the brain of my being, I feel it again, and I die a thousand deaths as one who has tasted love and found it has suddenly lost its savor, not understanding where it has disappeared.

A person is born with so much love and contentment in his soul, also a certain amount of wildness and desire that must cease to stay in the soul but come forth for glory and fulfillment. If this feeling cannot come forth but must be destined to live forever in darkness, it spreads throughout the soul and overwhelms it until it can no longer be contented but rises against its will to overpower the understanding of its being.

I think, and thoughts no longer help me. I remember, and memories no longer nourish this feeling that has gone within me. I speak of things that are dreary and unwanted, of things this feeling has feasted upon. I no longer try to control this hated and dreaded emotion but give way to its laughing triumphant feeling of satisfaction, for it has won its great battle for soul possession and I am lost.

In this poignant inner biography, the sensitive student of the human spirit can discern converging lines of intense anxiety of every quality. Participation in the unfolding pilgrimage of this woman, as well as that of many others like her, reveals the necessity of such concern for the birth of a new life of the spirit. When one works within the heavy pressures of a pastoral and teaching ministry, he comes to ask himself a basic question concerning the persons who seek his aid: " How desperate is this person in his own eyes? "

The pastoral counselor who takes this desperation seriously needs also to develop simultaneously a concept of the creative force of such anxiety in the birth of a new self. Thus he approaches personality with an integrated, synoptic perspective in his pastoral care of confused people. The more he does this, the more he realizes that pastoral counseling has its own unique characteristics. Much of what has been said and done in the field of pastoral counseling attempts to manipulate finite people by finite techniques toward finite objectives. It does not take into consideration the fact that finitude itself is a problem of anxiety to the counselee. Nor does it take into consideration his need for the regeneration of life as its source as a prerequisite to the redirection of life toward its goals. When pastoral counselors follow such superficial patterns, they overlook the "pearl of great value" which has been committed to them in the gospel. At best, they cast the pearl before the people, who react as if they had no more identity in the universe than sheep at best or swine at worst. As Spafford Ackerly, M.D., of Norton Psychiatric Clinic in Louisville, Kentucky, has said, "The purpose of religion is the creation of new life, the development of feeling tone, and the regeneration of psychic energy."

Such regeneration is evident in the following account of a particular person who came to a pastor with a definite burden of anxiety. She was desperate. A careful preliminary interview composed the formal inception of the counseling relationship. During this formal inception, the character of the anxiety was revealed and evaluated. The forty-year-old mother of four children was pressed with the stringent economic anxiety of living on the salary of her husband, who worked long hours and brought work home with him at night in order to make a little more money. She felt life closing in on her with a poverty of meaning and a sense of hopelessness as to where all this monotony would lead. All the while she hungered for some deeper revealing of happiness. She was overwhelmed with grief because her mother had recently died, and her father had remarried. Her father's second marriage was in severe straits because he was a hopeless alcoholic. He could not care for the younger sister of the counselee, and she had to take the sixteen-year-old sister to enable her to live safely from the threats of the father. Furthermore, the anxiety was an anxiety of grief because she had done certain things that made her feel so guilty that her life was one continuous burden of the anxiety of grief and guilt. She felt alienated from her best self and from clear communication with God and those whose understanding she needed most. Nevertheless, this woman had a remarkable sense of humor, a bold desire to know herself as God knew her, and a realistic desire to be a better wife and mother. In the following account she tells in her own words the story of the struggle of her soul. By her specific permission use is made here of her account as she wrote it:

Something very wonderful has happened to me and I am attempting to describe it on paper in order to understand it better.

Three facts are uppermost in my mind at this point: the fact that my pastor prayed that the "inner person" would be strengthened; the fact that the "inner me" was struggling for strength; and the fact that at the same time I read the right book. I am very much convinced that I was in God's hands throughout this experience.

The book was *Neurosis and Human Growth,* by Karen Horney, M.D. Right now I feel that it is the most exciting book I have ever read. (Remember, I have never studied psychology before.) The basic premise of the book is that man by nature strives toward self-realization, and the fact that inherent in him are constructive forces toward that end was thrilling to me. How could I determine what these forces in me were and how could I free them?

So, then I read about the real self and the factors that cultivate it. I read about the adverse conditions which prevent its growth. I read of the devices we use to avoid or defend ourselves from situations we cannot cope with by being ourselves. One then becomes alienated from his real self. The anxiety that results seeks to recover an identity with the "idealized self" we have created. I read of "the search for glory" on that basis and the nature of its repercussions. I learned about compulsive acts, and why they are compulsive. I learned the difference between a basic propensity to develop given potentialities and a neurotic search for glory through neurotic ambition, the need for perfection, the need for vindictive triumph, and the need for self-idealization.

I remember the *basic anxiety* I read about. I experienced all these things in my own life: not being accepted as I was and yearning to

be otherwise; aims for superiority over anything and anybody. My
own solutions alternated between obnoxious aggressiveness and placat-
ing overhumility and a great, great desire to please by being " super-
sweet." I am impressed with the fact that my real self grew as much
as it did. I attribute this to the fact that my mother was the unneu-
rotic person she was and that there was a great deal of religious train-
ing in my younger life. (I was sent to Sunday school, to young people's conferences, and was very active in such.) A lot of my activities
were motivated by half-neurotic aims, but *some* of the real meaning
got through to me. It occurs to me that you decided there was evidence that my real self was a going concern in spite of the neurotic
trends that were there also. Yes? No?

To follow the book farther, I recognized my own use of neurotic
claims to further my illusions. I was sure of many things I was entitled to from other people in particular and society and life in general. For example, being treated like an adult even if I behaved like
a brat, being considered a " wonderful wife and mother " when in
reality I did better than some and not so good as others. I could go
on much farther. This section was very revealing to me.

" The Tyranny of the Should," as Horney calls it, is a phenomenon
I know. I should be calm at all times; I should be very, very intelli-
gent; I should be sweet and a friend to everybody at all times; I
should never be blue; I should never be sick; I should never complain — etc., etc., etc. Violating these coercive " Shoulds " is followed
by self-hate. *I* could write a book on that one. The feeling that " me
as I really am " is all that stands between this wonderful superior (yet
humble) creation I *could* be if everybody else co-operated! My result-
ant misery and tension I tried to minimize by blaming others, and
hanging onto my illusions, literally, for dear life!

When I read her [Horney's] more detailed discussions of the different types of neurotic solutions I kept trying to " type " myself in
spite of her clear statement to the effect that such typing is rarely
possible. I finally got to the " I have done this " and " I never did this "
stage. Frequently, the angel on my shoulder would say, " Halt " when
I was too sure that this particular description did not fit me. Frequently I had to rearrange my thoughts. The section on the " Self-
effacing Solution," particularly regarding " morbid dependency," was
very illuminating. Needless to say a need for dependence was the
situation that brought me to you for help in the first place. When
Horney referred to the great amount of subjective unhappiness involved in this setup, I wanted to say amen,

One thought that keeps coming back to me (maybe it is dictated by neurotic pride) is that the dependency in my most unhappy relationships in life alternated between the different people concerned. Or maybe it didn't. I was certainly the obsessed one. The things the book said that I want to hold onto about the results of having lived through such an experience went like this — *Provided she can mobilize sufficient constructive forces during her struggle and has matured through the real suffering involved, plain ordinary honesty with self and efforts to get on her own feet can go far to attaining a measure of inner freedom.* Horney was concerned with the possibility of outgrowing the causes and effects of such situations without psychoanalysis. However, Horney did not mention the particular advantage I have. I have a friend and I have a God and the three of us are doing very well. Incidentally the idea of using a crutch no longer humiliates me. I am very grateful for it. Also, I am no longer " scared to death " to be friends with people. This is a help, believe me.

In spite of recognizing myself many times in Horney's book, I couldn't help being amazed that I had gotten along as well *as I had being about one fourth alive*. Pastor, you say, " Being away from the land of the living "; Horney says being " alienated from yourself "; Horney says the " real self "; you say " the inner person." As I recognized myself and my neurotic trends the most remarkable thing happened. My excessive irritability and inordinate bad temper are becoming much, much less of a problem. My husband, my children, and my sister are all aware of it. But I don't think they realize *why* life is so much sweeter. My younger sister has hugged me often in the last few weeks. I wonder if she has any idea why she wants to and why she feels free to. I could say a great deal about my relationship with my husband. It already has ranged from very affectionate to his being very critical of my housekeeping, cooking, etc. I think he may be realizing that he can express his natural grievances without having a battle or such. Since I do not have to be the only perfect person in the world and since my self-respect does not depend on never being criticized, I can take being told how to cook, etc. I even profit by it occasionally.

I do not feel that I'll never have a problem again, but I do feel that they will be problems — not the functionings of a neurotic solution to living. I expect time will simmer down this glorious " lit up " *feeling of being alive* I have now. No, I don't either. There are resources that will maintain it, and I will use them to that end. I am learning the difference in loving God and feeling sentimental toward him. He has loved me.

I couldn't stop without mentioning that I have acquired a very healthy respect for Satan — a Satan who leads people to provide environments for their children conducive to this entire picture of alienation from the real self. It is truly a vicious circle. These estrangements from reality perpetuate themselves. It appears to be fiendishly a perfect setup for the propagation of evil.

It would be perfect but for one factor. God can destroy it, overcome it, or render it impotent. And I believe he can use the knowledge of it in his own plans as the wisdom of the serpent which Jesus recommended. Incidentally, it would appear that a man of God who underestimates the power of these neurotic factors is playing into the Devil's hands (do you capitalize " devil "?). Alienated from myself, I am unable to worship God. If this is true of me, I dare to think it is true for many others.

After having talked *about* God a good bit, I would talk *to* him. My prayer for a pastor would be that many other people will be helped through such understanding and kindness as I have received from my pastor. Most important of all, my pastor's closeness to God is evident, not in his much speaking, but in the way I have been helped. I pray that God will find others to work this way for him. Amen.

This frank personal biography of a person who felt herself to be only one fourth alive, and through the dynamic birth of a new life she felt gloriously lighted up with the feeling of once again being alive. More often such persons are relatively normal individuals who are burdened with a restlessness over the passing of the days of their years, a feeling of alienation from God and their associates because of both grief and sin, and unreasonable needs for perfection which had been taught them. Here the counseling pastor encounters people who need more than superficial guidance. They need a secure relationship to a pastoral counselor in a situation that extends over as many as a dozen or more conferences. The pastor moves through the experience of becoming a real person with them. Actually this is the essence of the conversion experience, theologically associated with the concept of regeneration. The counselees with whom the author has worked usually report that they feel that they are new persons, that they were dead and now alive, lost and now found. They speak of their old self as being in the past tense. They usually do not give it a theological name at first. Nevertheless, they begin to talk about a new basis for living, to be concerned about their prayer life in an interpersonal fellowship with God, and to enter into a sense of security they have not known before.

This person in particular perceived her experience as *both* a theological experience of redemption *and* an emotional experience of healing. One moves with her as she takes upon herself the limitations of her life, dies to sin, and is born into a new being in God. Whereas no specific reference to the cross appears in her description, the inherent reality of the cross is being re-enacted. As she put it, not in her much speaking, but in the effectual changes that really took place.

II. Concepts of Psychotherapy Relevant to Understanding the Anxiety of the Cross

One needs to be exceptionally careful not to take the concepts of modern psychotherapists out of the settings of their typically naturalistic presuppositions and apply them to spiritual realities which assume the activity of a personal God in the affairs of men. However, the phenomena which the psychotherapists describe empirically may be said to be the observable manifestations of the inner spiritual activity of God. The Christian, therefore, can draw some inferences as to the psychology of religious experience by careful study of modern psychotherapy.

The psychotherapists have been unusually penetrating in their insights concerning the anxiety contingent with the birth of a new life, which might be theologically described as the anxiety of the cross. One of the most provocative writers among them at this point is Otto Rank. His book *Truth and Reality* includes a chapter entitled " The Birth of Individuality," in which he defines the " conflictual separation of the individual from the mass, undertaken and continued at every step of development into the new, . . . as the never completed birth of individuality." This experience is fraught with productive tension and " from the birth of the child from the mother, beyond the birth of the individual from the mass, to the birth of the creative work from the individual, and finally to the birth of knowledge from the work." All this corresponds somehow "to the biological contrast of procreation and birth." (Otto Rank, *Truth and Reality*, pp. 219, 220.)

Such anxiety is the precondition of creativity in the thought of Rank; the "conflictual separation" is a tension-producing relationship. According to his teachings, this conflict takes into account the finitude of both the counselor and the counselee in the process of therapy in that time is a vital and limiting factor. Through the technique of "end setting" for the resolution of the patient's difficulty, the counselor and the counselee come to grips with the fact that neither of them is more than human, and that the birth of the spirit has its day of consummation also. The purpose of this end setting is to further and intensify therapy, to strengthen and invigorate the will to a new life in the patient. Rank says:

"Once in a discussion I gave a spontaneous definition of end setting as a 'last hour' prolonged. . . . In the light of my present conception, this 'last hour' contains a deeper meaning, as the patient actually reacts in case of an ending not prepared for, as if his last hour had come. In a prolonged end situation he learns not only to die gradually, which we have recognized as a fundamental life principle, but he also learns gradually to live." (*Will Therapy*, p. 193.)

Another psychotherapist, Harry M. Tiebout, calls this kind of learning the result of "the act of surrender." He has written careful articles on the effectiveness of this act of surrender in the care and cure of alcoholics. This act comes at a moment in time when "the unconscious forces of defiance and grandiosity actually cease to function." (Harry M. Tiebout, "The Act of Surrender in the Treatment of the Alcoholic," *Pastoral Psychology*, March, 1950, p. 37.) This occurs upon the inner, unconscious acceptance of reality. With it comes the release from tension, the relaxation that ensues with freedom from strain and conflict. A vital change is effected in the life of the alcoholic which Tiebout frankly identifies as conversion. In another article (Harry M. Tiebout, "Conversion as a Psychological Phenomenon (in the Treatment of the Alcoholic)," in *Pastoral Psychology,* April, 1951, p. 29), Tiebout speaks of this experience of conversion as "the breaking through of a wall" whereby the patient comes closer to life and is enabled to feel freer to meet life. The breaking through releases power, a sensation of inner strength and freedom which comes when people find themselves liberated or released from their psychological wall." (*Ibid.*)

The self-examinations provoked by intense suffering and anxiety preceding such a rebirth often are, as Paracelsus said about every illness, a "purgatorial fire." The comfort of Thomas a Kempis is appropriate at this point. He said: "When thou art ill at ease and troubled is the time when thou art nearest unto blessing." Anton Boisen (see his *The Exploration of the Inner World*) has often said that this concern is like unto an acute fever which heals at the same time it hurts. The symbol of the ancient belief of the Jews that healing took place in the pool of Bethzatha at the troubling of the water is appropriate here. Apparently there is no healing creativity without anxiety, the troubling of the waters of the spirit!

III. A BIBLICAL AND THEOLOGICAL PERSPECTIVE OF THE ANXIETY OF THE CROSS

A clear pattern of interpretation of the experience of faith in the New Testament reveals the anxiety of the cross in the message of the gospel. Jesus knew this kind of anxiety in the greatest measure by reason of his own life of pure faith. In the severe confrontation of the reality of his cross, as has been seen, his soul was troubled. (John 12:27.) This troubling was spiritually creative in quality. Luke describes the experience of anxiety under which Jesus labored so creatively in the following manner:

"I have a baptism to be baptized with; and how I am constrained until it is accomplished!" (Luke 12:50.)

Moffatt translates the same passage as follows:

"I have a baptism to undergo —
what tension I suffer, till it is over!"

This travail of the soul is characterized by an impending necessity of that which is to come, and a feeling of the suspension of all other issues of life as the whole organism martials itself around this life crisis. A further illustration of this anxiety is evident in the experience of the apostle Paul. In II Cor. 4:8 he speaks of being troubled on every side, or afflicted in every way, but not distressed, completely straitened, or hemmed in in the narrowness of existence. Drawing his thought from similar descriptive words in Rom. 8:22, also, Paul speaks of the "whole creation . . . groaning in travail together until now." He adds a personal note and says:

"And not only the creation, but we ourselves, who have the first fruits of the Spirit, groan inwardly as we wait for adoption as sons, the redemption of our bodies. For in this hope we were saved. Now hope that is seen is not hope. For who hopes for what he sees? But if we hope for what we do not see, we wait for it with patience."

The word "groaning" here means the eager expectation of the creation which anxiously awaits the advent of the new creation in Christ. This anxiety characterizes the universal fellowship of suffering; it is the prelude to great spiritual productivity, inexpressibly profound; Christians bear it together as they earnestly expect the redemption of the world.

The concept of faith as involving the anxiety of the cross expressed in Paul's teaching here relates directly to the classical definition of faith found in Heb. 11:1: "Now faith is the assurance of things hoped for, the conviction of things not seen." Faith in this context may be interpreted as the capacity to bear the anxiety of thrusting one's life forward into the uncharted and unknown without shrinking back. In other words, the righteous live by faith. The birth, realization, and preservation of the soul is by faith, the opposite of which is the shrinking back to the safety zones of freedom from the adventure of the cross. To shrink back is to be destroyed. To have faith is to keep one's soul. (Heb. 10:38,39.)

The roll call of the faith community following these passages in the eleventh chapter of Hebrews is a cherishing reminder of

those persons who did not shrink back. They were capable of
bearing the anxiety preludes to God's revelation of himself.
They could stand the anxiety of not knowing exactly where
they were going at all times, and with fortitude were enabled
to refuse " to accept release, that they might rise again to a better life."

The antithesis of these brilliant heroes of faith appears in the
shrinking back of the rich young man who came to Jesus. He
had fixed himself upon that which was seen; he could not bear
the anxiety of a creative faith; he sought release from this trouble-
some young Rabbi whose love stirred within him the anxiety that
always prefaces a new life about to be born from within. He
shrank back from the brink of the unknown and preferred the security of the success that he had already achieved, the wealth upon
which he had a tight grip, and the narrowed existence of his
finite idolatries. One might suppose he turned later to some cult
of reassurance that lulled him to believe that his success in life
was a *sure* sign of God's favor. Today he would probably have
turned to a barbiturate religion that soothed him away from the
necessity of a cross, a new birth, and the courage of the unknown.
He may have bought and worn out books on the " power of positive thinking," " peace of mind," and " how to stop worrying and
start living." He would certainly need these, because in fleeing
from the anxiety of the cross he had shrunk back into the narrow
resting place of a smug safety and under the shivering covers of
the insatiable worship of finitude! His sense of separation from
the young " pioneer of our faith " must have been widened to
despair when he later heard about the ignominious death of the
Rabbi who had challenged him to follow him.

Abraham exemplifies the kind of faith that courageously encounters the anxiety of cross-bearing in response to the promise
of God for a new life. The author of Hebrews describes him:
" By faith Abraham obeyed when he was called to go out to a
place which he was to receive as an inheritance; and he went out,
not knowing where he was to go " (Heb. 11:8). He did not have
a ceiled and plastered house in a safe social bracket, carefully

subdivided and zoned away from the threats of people different
from himself. Rather, he lived in tents, " for he looked forward
to the city which has foundations, whose builder and maker is
God."

Lewis J. Sherrill has given a brilliant exegesis of the book of
Hebrews in his volume *The Struggle of the Soul,* in which he
expresses the experience of faith in the " emergence of the
dynamic self " into vital relationship with God and the Christian community. He points out that life can be either a treadmill
of monotony with no regard for the birth of a new self, a saga
of conflict in the wresting of a selfhood from an unwilling world,
or a pilgrimage of discovery in which the selfhood of an individual is received through the grace of having been accepted by God.
Essentially these three symbols indicated three ways of handling
anxiety: by apathy and indifference, by hostility and defensiveness,
or by grace through faith.

Sören Kierkegaard, in his book *The Sickness Unto Death,* de-
votes the whole treatise to the problems of anxiety or despair
associated with " becoming a self before God." The classical
theologians have given an ex post facto treatment of the problem
of the new birth (which is in essence the topic of conversation in
this discussion of the anxiety of the cross). However, these theologians have been less complete in giving a detailed treatment of
the process of the birth of a new self. Kierkegaard does just this
in his entire authorship in one way or another. His writing is
devoted to the treatment of the problem of " what it means to
become a Christian." (Sören Kierkegaard, *The Point of View,*
translated by Walter Lowrie, p. 22. Oxford University Press,
1939.) He dramatizes the very courage to which reference has
been made concerning Abraham when he says: " The Christian
heroism . . . is to venture wholly to be oneself, as an individual
man, alone before the face of God." (Sören Kierkegaard, *The
Sickness Unto Death,* p. 4.) In the ensuing pages, Kierkegaard
then gives a penetrating analysis of the qualities of anxiety that
grasp a person who would become a self before God. As Madden
has accurately said: " The true Christian does not cover over the

fears of death with wishes (as Freud said)." (Myron Madden, *The Contributions of Sören Kierkegaard to a Christian Psychology*, Unpublished Doctoral Dissertation, p. 32. Southern Baptist Theological Seminary, 1950.) " He actually faces death, . . . the worst calamity of ' nature ' and ' culture,' without too much perturbation because he has learned to fear something greater, i.e., spiritual death." (Sören Kierkegaard, *The Sickness Unto Death*, p. 14.)

This death is what Paul Tillich has called " the threat of nonbeing." The action of faith, then, is the affirmation of anxiety of the cross and the birth of a new self as an alternative to the anxiety of not becoming a self before God. Kierkegaard says that this anxiety is of three different orders:

" Despair is a sickness of the spirit, in the self, and so it may assume a triple form: in despair at not being conscious of having a self (despair improperly so-called); despair at not willing to be oneself; in despair at willing to be oneself." (*Ibid.*, p. 17.)

The despair at not being conscious of having a self is irrelevant to considerations here. But the shrinking back or not willing to be a self is highly relevant to the conditions of the person who has withdrawn from reality after having been caught in an either-or situation between the possibilities revealed to him in his imagination and the necessities hemming him in as he attempts to relate himself to the real world about him. When a person begins to react to the sense of personal failure, therefore, it is not surprising to see him come up with an oversymbolization of his nearness to the end of *his* world. Or, he may feel that life is no longer worth living.

The person who avoids these kinds of anxiety does so by becoming apathetic or openly defensive toward them. He may erect false structures of safety, retreat to an unrealistic zone, a false security, protecting himself from the necessity of becoming a self. As the impending necessity of a new life comes upon him, it is " as if a man fled from a lion, and a bear met him; or went into the house and leaned with his hand against the wall, and a serpent bit him " (Amos 5:19). He runs from the creative anxiety involved in becoming a self before God, and the threat of non-being meets him. In other words, he avoids the cross. Then he goes home and is bitten by his own meaninglessness, emptiness, and boredom. Kierkegaard is right, then, when he says that the Christian " acquires a courage . . . by learning fear for the still more dreadful." (Sören Kierkegaard, *The Sickness Unto Death*, p. 14.) The Christian commitment knows how to be afraid of the kind of nonbeing caricatured by Margaret Elizabeth Austin in her poem " Charlie Sapiens ":

> " Man is the only animal that keeps
> A place for everything, with nothing in it;
> Vainly he yearns for order; chaos creeps
> Higher around his body by the minute;
> His mind a magpie nest; his fingers thumbs,
> He builds on sand and plants upon the rock,
> And thereupon, as brisk as morning, comes
> Efficiently to work at eight o'clock.

> " The lost knife and the empty gun are his;
> His the rash footsteps and the plunge to terror;
> Yet his the mind whose workman's pride it is
> To add long columns up without an error.
> By faulty balance sheets is he unmanned
> Whose birth is incident and death unplanned."

(Published by the Alumni Association of Montana State College, Bozeman, Montana, in *Arrowy Time*. Used by permission.)

Of course, from a theological point of view, any discussion of the creative anxiety of the cross must include the contribution of Paul Tillich in his book *The Courage to Be*. He perceived certain types of anxiety as being inescapable, and to avoid them is to lose one's humanity. The courage to take this inescapable anxiety upon oneself assumes three main forms: the courage to be as a part of a larger whole, the courage to stand alone, and the courage to accept the fact that man is carried by the creative power of being in which every creature participates. He says that the neurotic person is one who is more highly sensitive to the threat of self-destruction, of nonbeing. He retires to a " castle and defends it with all means of psychological resistance against attack,"

either from reality or from the counselor. The neurotic handling of anxiety becomes evident as the inability to take one's
existential anxiety upon one's self.

But such anxiety cannot be borne alone, and serves to make
the confrontation of God all the more imperative. The impending necessity of such a cross thrusts man into the very presence
of God. He stands with fear and trembling in the terror striking
awareness that he is man and not God. His dependence upon the
providence of God in his economic anxiety, his finite weakness
manifest in the anxiety of his creatureliness, the pressure of his
sense of estrangement in his grief, the uncleanness and feeling of
condemnation in his awareness of sin, the impotence of his having kept the law as a means of salvation, and the pointlessness of
his feeling of cunning and cleverness in trying to be indifferent
to God — all these come to a crescendo of " sheer terror " which
might be called " holy dread."

CHAPTER

8

THE ANXIETY OF
THE CROSS AND HOLY DREAD

I. THE ULTIMATE DIMENSION OF ANXIETY

The ultimate dimension of anxiety stands forth in an individual or group's confrontation of God as the Holy One. His holiness creates an intense awareness of the whole gamut of anxieties described here. At the same time, the secure love of a righteous God undergirds the anxious person with a humble confidence in the acceptance he receives in the new life from God. The character of God is manifested in the anxious response of man in his presence as he eagerly awaits the reconciliation which proceeds forth from the mind of God in Christ. This anxious response may be accurately called "holy dread."

Holy dread, or the reverential fear of God, stands forth in the Biblical accounts as the distinctly religious anxiety of the one who meets God face to face. Anxiety "before God" is a compound anxiety; a spectrum of the anxieties that have been described in the foregoing pages intermingles in holy dread. In its brilliance, fire and light are often mentioned as the symbols of the "appearance of the brightness round about" (Ezek. 1:28). Speaking figuratively, one might say that this brilliance gathers up the whole rainbow of anxieties, making them clearer in their separate detail and then obscuring them in the oneness of the worship anxiety to be discussed here.

The Old Testament saga of spiritual encounters between men and God is full of descriptions of this kind of spiritual anxiety. At the lowest level of revelation, the holiness of God is perceived in the Old Testament as "a mysterious power, somewhat akin to electricity, which automatically becomes contagious and kills instantly not alone through contact but even by mere sight." For instance, in Ex. 29:37, it is said that "whatever touches the altar shall become holy," and in Num. 4:15–20 the idea is set forth that to touch or even to see "the holy things even for a moment" is to die. Obviously, the fear of death and other lesser forms of finitude anxiety are projected into the fetishlike character of the sacramental objects. (Robert H. Pfeiffer, *Introduction to the Old Testament*, p. 270. Harper & Brothers, 1941.)

A more personal and less mechanical manifestation of holy dread is evident in the divine-human encounter of Moses in Ex. 3:5 and Josh. 5:15. Both of them were told to remove their shoes, for the place on which they were standing was holy. Ezekiel (Ezek. 1:26 to 2:3) says that when he saw "the appearance of the likeness of the glory of the Lord," he fell upon his face and "heard the voice of one speaking." He says that the "Spirit entered into" him and set him "upon his feet." The first thrust of fear and dread was relieved, and the confidence of the prophet in the presence of the Holy One of Israel was established. Immediately afterward the needs of the people of Israel became the object of conversation. In the subsequent story (ch. 11:13 ff.) he tells how, when Pelatiah died, he, Ezekiel, once again fell upon his face and cried with a loud voice to God, asking: "Ah Lord God! wilt thou make a full end of the remnant of Israel?" Apparently his concern over the shortness of the life of his people converged to make this bereavement experience one of real confrontation of the Eternal.

Isaiah was filled with awe, or holy dread, as he learned of the true nature of Yahweh:

> "Holy, holy, holy is the Lord of hosts;
> the whole earth is full of his glory."

Bewer says that "at the vision of holiness Isaiah was shaken with fear. In the swift realization of his own sinfulness he cried out in utter dismay. He had seen the divine mystery, he knew that he must die." (Julius A. Bewer, *The Literature of the Old Testament,* revised edition, p. 100. Columbia University Press, 1938.) Once again a sense of forgiveness and spiritual cleansing and strengthening took place whereby the prophet was enabled to see the needs of his people as well as to feel his own. Every quality of anxiety blends together in the creative thrust of Isaiah's spirit in the highly symbolic experience described in Isa. 6:1 ff. His experience with holy dread or spiritual anxiety translated the concept of holiness from that of a primitive untouchableness "into majestic greatness and exclusive sovereignty" which gave the idea "a baptism into moral meanings." (Harry Emerson Fosdick, *A Guide to Understanding the Bible,* p. 211. Harper & Brothers, 1938.)

Some would assume that all elements of fear and dread fade from worship once one crosses from the Old Testament into the New Testament confrontations of the living God. The element of dread or the feeling of threat in the presence of God is not alien to the Christian revelation of God, however. The consistent relief of the fear, nevertheless, predominantly characterizes the self-revelatory character of God as love in Jesus Christ our Lord, casting out fear.

Jesus again and again sensed the fear and apprehensiveness which others manifested in his presence. He revealed the character or nature of God in the way he met the profound sense of dread in his followers. The two most acutely dreadful experiences, from the point of view of the disciples, both, interestingly enough, involved the apostle Peter. The first is described in Luke 5:1-11, where, after the heavy catch of fish had been hauled in, Peter said to the Lord, "Depart from me, for I am a sinful man, O Lord." A keen sense of mission on the part of Peter, James, and John arose out of this deep self-confrontation occasioned by the awareness of the nature of our Lord. "They left everything and followed him."

The most dramatic example of holy dread, however, was the occasion of the walking of Jesus on the waves of the sea. Three of the four Evangelists record this story (Mark 6:45-52; Matt.

14:23–33; John 6:15–21). The Matthew account says that they
"were terrified" and "cried out for fear." Jesus reassured them
that it was he and that they should take heart and have no fear.
A similar sense of terror took hold of them when they were
crossing the sea "to the other side," and when he reassured them
and quieted the waves, "they were filled with awe" (Mark 4:41),
a kind of reverential fear.

Other examples of holy dread in the presence of Jesus can be
cited. The woman who had a "flow of blood for twelve years"
and touched his garment came to him "in fear and trembling."
Likewise his disciples were afraid at the death of Jairus' daughter.
Jesus felt it necessary, therefore, to say, "Do not fear; only believe, and she shall be well" (Luke 8:50).

The perfect love of Jesus was undoubtedly a threat to those
who were his enemies, "for they feared him, because all the
multitude was astonished at his teaching" (Mark 11:18). John
the Baptist's presence was also awe-striking inasmuch as Mark
says of him, "Herod feared John, knowing that he was a righteous and holy man. . . ." This may also have been some of the
incense of the genuinely awe-inspiring holiness of which Paul
was confident when he said:

"But thanks be to God, who in Christ always leads us in triumph,
and through us spreads the fragrance of the knowledge of him everywhere. For we are the aroma of Christ to God among those who are
being saved and among those who are perishing, to one a fragrance
from death to death, to the other a fragrance from life to life. Who is
sufficient for these things?" (II Cor. 2:14–16.)

Even in the utmost heights of his beatific vision of the holiness
of God, however, the apostle Paul experienced the anxiety of his
own creatureliness in the thorn in the flesh, given unto him to
remind him of his humanity and that he not be "too elated"
(II Cor. 12:1 ff.). Paul's basic acceptance of his humanity apparently refined dread and anxiety from his relationship to God. He
expresses the infinite holiness without any sense of fear in
Rom. 11:33:

"O the depth of the riches and wisdom and knowledge of God! How unsearchable are his judgments and how inscrutable his ways!"

When anxiety takes on the character of an ultimate concern and gains the personal reference in self-confrontation of God, then the presence of the living God overwhelms man's sense of holy dread by the power of *agape,* which casts out fear. The response of God to the cry of man for salvation is always healing and relief of fear. As the hymn puts it:

> "'Twas grace that taught my heart to fear,
> And grace my fears relieved."

The brunt of Fosdick's discussion on the idea of the holy is right when he points out that that which in the lowest stages of human encounter with God appears as *horror and terror of the holy* becomes the inexpressible gift of fellowship with God in the Holy Spirit through the love of Christ. (*Op. cit.,* p. 213 ff.) The author of The Letter to the Hebrews underlines this shift from the Old Testament to the gospel witness when he says:

"For you have not come to what may be touched, a blazing fire, and darkness, and gloom, and a tempest, and the sound of a trumpet, and a voice whose words made the hearers entreat that no further messages be spoken to them. For they could not endure the order that was given, 'If even a beast touches the mountain, it shall be stoned.' Indeed, so terrifying was the sight that Moses said, 'I tremble with fear.' But you have come . . . to Jesus, the mediator of a new covenant." (Heb. 12:18 ff.)

Even earlier the writer of Hebrews says that men can "with confidence draw near to the throne of grace" to "receive mercy and find grace to help in time of need" (Heb. 4:16).

Such a transition calls for an actual "working through" of the specific ways in which anxiety in all its forms distorts the knowledge of God's grace and presence, however. This process is aided and implemented by an indwelling power of God himself. The power of holy dread is manifest in the need for a God whom man can worship without fear of destruction, and yet whose place man cannot take or find an adequate substitute for in his petty scheme of self-omnipotence and puny idolatries. This seems to be the paradox which Paul is teaching in his contrast between "high-mindedness" and "fear" in Rom. 11:20–22. The Revised Standard Version reads: "So do not become proud, but stand in awe. . . . Note then the kindness and the severity of God." Apparently man need fear or dread the God our Lord Jesus Christ *only when he attempts to take his place!* This is the basic sin. As Tillich has said, "Religiously speaking, sin is the attempt of man to fulfill his human possibilities in an unlimited and undetermined way."

The tension between man's high-mindedness and his awe in the presence of God calls for continued fellowship with God, the experience of repentance, and the development of a wide and deep social passion. These three phases of spiritual maturity are obvious in the second chapter of Paul's letter to the Philippians. He says:

"God has highly exalted him [Jesus] and bestowed on him the name which is above every name, that at the name of Jesus every knee should bow, in heaven and on earth and under the earth, and every tongue confess that Jesus Christ is Lord, to the glory of the Father" (ch. 2:9–11).

The recognition and confession of Jesus as Lord centers all of life upon the supreme Person of persons in the hierarchy of loves of an individual. Identification with him and participation in his cross strikes at the deepest sources of creating change within an individual personality, and the deepest need of the worshiper is to be like the Lord Jesus Christ. As Paul describes his own experience, he says:

"I have been crucified with Christ; it is no longer I who live, but Christ who lives in me; and the life I now live in the flesh I live by faith in the Son of God, who loved me and gave himself for me" (Gal. 2:20).

This works more in the unconscious realms of personality than in the more superficial areas of imitations of conscious perceptions of what Jesus would be like if he were a contemporary human being. This deepest and most selfless kind of relatedness is described in Paul's words as follows:

" And we all, with unveiled face, beholding the glory of the Lord, are being changed into his likeness from one degree of glory to another; for this comes from the Lord who is the Spirit " (II Cor. 3:18).

Then again, the writer of I John underlines the fact that this is a love relationship whereby this transformation of personality takes place:

" See what love the Father has given us, that we should be called children of God; and so we are. ... Beloved, we are God's children now; it does not yet appear what we shall be, but we know that when he appears we shall be like him, for we shall see him as he is." (I John 3:1,2.)

As Oswald McCall has so aptly said, men gather themselves to the images they love.

" And there in your mind and spirit they will leave with you their distilled essence, sweet as honey or bitter as gall, and you will grow into their likeness because their nature will be in you. . . . For men become like that which they love, and the name thereof is written on their brows." (Oswald McCall, *The Hand of God,* pp. 100, 101. Harper & Brothers, 1939.)

Such a worship calls for a reverential fear and sense of awe in worship. The achievement of this kind of relationship to God necessitates personal discipline and a sense of dependence upon God at the same time:

" Therefore, my beloved, . . . work out your own salvation with fear and trembling; for God is at work in you, both to will and to work for his good pleasure " (Phil. 2:12,13).

The radical difference between men and the Lord Jesus Christ cannot be overcome without travail of soul, a renunciation of all that is an impediment to growth, and the hope of eternity in which to accomplish his will.

II. Empirical Descriptions of Holy Dread

One of the contemporary psychotherapists, Harry S. Sullivan, has had a good deal to say about an empirical description of holy dread in his discussions of *uncanny emotions*. He calls it a "sudden, intense, all-encompassing anxiety . . . hinted at by four words in our language — awe, dread, loathing, and horror." He likens it to the experience of size and vastness, such as seeing the Grand Canyon. He says that "one is, as it were, lifted utterly out of the context of life and is profoundly impressed." If one should happen to go into a church of great proportions, the sense of awe may take on "the thought of the nature and actual presence of deity."

The experience of awe is least sudden and least paralyzing of the various shades of uncanny emotion. Dread itself, loathing, and horror "seem to be of the essence of sudden attacks of all-paralyzing anxiety." These tend to arise out of conflict between what Sullivan calls the good-me, the bad-me, and the not-me in the self-system of an individual, and the sense of uncanny arises, Sullivan feels, from the confrontation of unacceptable manifestations of the self-system which an individual has disowned up until this time. (Harry S. Sullivan, *The Interpersonal Theory of Psychiatry,* pp. 315, 316. W. W. Norton & Company, Inc., 1953.) He points out that at the same time these uncanny emotions are revolting in a sense, they are also *fascinating* in another sense, and one's attention is drawn to them. They may take on the character of abhorrent cravings as in the case of the eruption of homosexual cravings in some persons. Panic and upheaval may easily be the result of such eruptions. "The far side of these panicky instances may be anything from terror to great religious exaltation." (*Ibid.,* p. 327.)

Another psychologist, Werner Wolff, in what he calls "a psychological analysis of the words, symbols, and beliefs of the Bible," calls attention to the fact that the holiness of God in the Biblical account represents the ultimate forces of creation and the ultimate forces of destruction at one and the same time.

"The Holy is the polar energy which can heal or destroy, from without in the forces of nature, or from within, in the soul. It is the force that moves to continuous renewal, which consists in the alternation of destroying and creating, of dying and being born, as Jesus says

142 ANXIETY IN CHRISTIAN EXPERIENCE

(John 12:24): 'Except a grain of wheat fall into the earth and die, it abideth by itself alone; but if it die it beareth much fruit.'" (Werner Wolff, *Changing Concepts of the Bible*, p. 346. Hermitage House, Inc., 1951.)

Wolff's insights apparently draw a straight line of connection between the experience of worship and the resolution of the anxiety of the cross.

III. THE THEOLOGICAL UNDERSTANDING OF HOLY DREAD

However, the psychotherapeutic psychologists tend to become less and less clinically oriented as they begin to deal with the sense of dread. Rather, they become more speculative and poetic in their presentations. In fact the best statements of this kind of dread are to be found among the psychologically inclined philosophers and theologians. These men tend to view the element of fear in sacred reverence in something of the thought of Schleiermacher, who said that fear was "not only not religion itself, but . . . not even preparatory to it." (Friedrich Schleiermacher, *On Religion: Speeches to Its Cultured Despisers*, translated by John Oman, p. 65. Kegan, Paul, Trench, Trubner and Co., Ltd., London, 1893.) Rather, they feel that the sense of awe is freed of fear by love, and reaches its height in the contemplation of the laws of God which equally embrace all things. Such contemplation comes to the individual in beatific moments when, according to Schleiermacher, "in every life there is some moment, like the coruscation of baser metals, when, by the approach of something higher, or by some electric shock, it surpasses itself and stands on the highest pinnacle of its possibilities." (*Ibid.*, p. 75.)

Such optimism concerning human nature, however, overlooks the way in which the anxiety of finitude, of grief, of sin, and of the law complicate that certain moment of encounter when an individual's possibilities are set before him. Sören Kierkegaard is much more realistic than Schleiermacher, it seems, when he says in this connection:

"Dread is a qualification of the dreaming spirit, and as such has its place in psychology. . . . One almost never sees the concept dread dealt with in psychology, and I must therefore call attention to the fact that it is different from fear and similar concepts which refer to something definite, whereas dread is the reality of freedom as possibility anterior to possibility." (Sören Kierkegaard, *The Concept of Dread,* translated by Walter Lowrie, p. 38. Princeton University Press, 1944.)

Here Sören Kierkegaard correlates the concept of dread with the premonition of possibility — either creative or destructive (if one follows Werner Wolff) as a person becomes a self before God. Kierkegaard captures the essentially contradictory nature of dread in his further definition of it as a *"sympathetic antipathy and an antipathetic sympathy."* (Italics in original.) He makes note of how this understanding of dread is built into language in such thoughts as "sweet dread, a sweet feeling of apprehension, . . . a strange dread, a shrinking dread, etc." (*Ibid.*)

The more ultimate character of dread before the Holy One is set forth in Kierkegaard's discussion of "What It Means to Seek God." He accents the element of loneliness in dread when he says:

"If a man would have an essential understanding of his sin, he must understand it through being alone, just he alone, alone with the Holy One who knows all. This is the only true fear and trembling, only this is the true sorrow which the remembrance of God awakens in a man, this is the true repentance His love encourages. . . . A man . . . should never rely on its being the duty of some other man to convict him of being a sinner . . . *no man can see God without purity, and sin is impurity, and therefore no one can take cognizance of God without becoming a sinner."* (Sören Kierkegaard, *Thoughts on Crucial Situations in Human Life,* pp. 24, 25. Augsburg Publishing House, 1941.)

Augustine catches a meaning similar to that of Kierkegaard's in his prayer:

"What is it to me that men should hear my confessions as if it were they who were going to cure all my infirmities? People are curious to know the lives of others, but slow to correct their own. Why are they anxious to hear from me what I am, when they are unwilling to hear from thee what they are?" (*Augustine: Confessions and Enchiridion,* edited by Albert C. Outler, Volume VII, The Library of Christian Classics. The Westminster Press, 1955.)

Of course, all the witness of the foregoing pages is gathered up in the contribution of Rudolf Otto in his book *The Idea of the Holy.* He moves away from a rationalistic interpretation of the religious life toward a deeper evaluation of the nonrational categories of the spiritual experience. He picks up the creature feeling, to which reference has been made in the discussion of finitude anxiety. He analyzes the *mysterium tremendum* before which a person experiences *awfulness* and *urgency.* The *mysterium tremendum* provokes a competitive set of feelings in *fascination* and *repugnance* or *horror.* He becomes more specifically theological when he says that "the hard core of such experiences in their Christian form consists of the redemption from guilt and bondage to sin." (Rudolf Otto, *The Idea of the Holy,* translated by John W. Harvey, p. 37. Oxford University Press, 1946.) The real nature of such experiences is essentially ineffable, according to Otto. As Schleiermacher says, they are of " such sort and so rare, that whoever utters anything of it, must necessarily have had it, for nowhere could he have heard it" (*op. cit.,* p. 9). Even so, Otto says that the experience of the holy one "can neither proclaim in speech nor conceive in thought, but may know only by a direct and living experience" (Otto, *The Idea of the Holy,* p. 33). Words stammer brokenly from one's tongue as he attempts to describe this " feeling of peculiar dread " which " seizes upon a man with paralyzing effect" (*ibid.,* p. 14). The shuddering realization of the experience, however, defies description.

The ineffability of religious experience at its best occasions a kind of anxiety in and of itself of which we have not had much to say. This is what might be called the anxiety of communication. Moses bore this fearful sense of not knowing what to say, not being able to talk, and not being able to explain to others " who had sent him." Jesus was aware of this difficulty of explanation which would overcome his disciples when they were hauled into court to explain their relationship to him. He reassured them: "Do not be anxious how or what you are to say; for the Holy Spirit will teach you in that very hour what you ought to say" (Luke 12:11,12). Likewise, the apostle Paul was convinced that even though the description of the inner meaning of being a Christian was immeasurably difficult, the effort of communication should not be abandoned for unintelligibility, for it was better in his opinion to say five words with understanding than ten thousand words in tongues (I Cor. 14:19).

Otto, likewise, is more realistic than Schleiermacher in that he does not perceive the sense of holy dread as alien to religion at its best. He says that "the peculiar quality of the 'uncanny' and 'awful,' which survives with the quality of exaltedness and sublimity . . . softened though it is, does not disappear even on the highest level of all where the worship of God is at its purest. Its disappearance would be an essential loss. The 'shudder' reappears in a form ennobled beyond measure where the soul, held speechless, trembles inwardly to the farthest fiber of its being." (*The Idea of the Holy,* p. 17.) As Goethe puts it:

> " Awe is the best of man: howe'er the world's
> Misprizing of the feeling would prevent us,
> Deeply we feel, once gripped, the weird Portentous."
> (*Faust,* Second Part, Act I, Scene v.)

IV. The Anxiety of the Cross and Holy Dread in the Pastoral Context

Nevertheless, the objective of the divine action in the life of the worshiping person is, as has been said before, the casting out of fear and at the same time the discovery of the sovereignty of the love of God. Furthermore, the thoughts of Kierkegaard and Augustine are basically sound in that the anxiety aroused in true worship cannot be resolved except by Him who stimulated it, even the Holy One.

This is the fallacy of much that is set forth as psychotherapy and much more that is set forth as pastoral counseling also.

Within the depths of the anxiety of man there is an anxious depth that neither man himself nor his compeers for him can reach. As Augustine has said, the mists of sin fume up and overcase the heart and befog the brightness of love with lustfulness of finite aims. The clanking chain of mortality deafens the ear to the eternal. Following the rushing of our own tide, we foam with anxiety like a troubled sea. All human aids are but lawgivers and tutors to lead us to the threshold of our inmost being where we confront God alone in the convicting power of his Presence. The objective of this relationship in the mind of God, as revealed in Christ, is to take the fear out of dread, the sting out of death, and the corruptibility out of mortality. Job puts it this way:

> " For he is not a man, as I am, that I might answer him,
>   that we should come to trial together.
> There is no umpire between us,
>   who might lay his hand upon us both.
> Let him take his rod away from me,
>   and let not dread of him terrify me.
> Then I would speak without fear of him,
>   for I am not so in myself."
>
> (Job 9:32-35.)

There is a point at which counseling becomes meddling in the relationship of a man to his God, for there are some things which only he can settle with himself as he exists before God. This is the basic wisdom of a person-centered kind of counseling which is built upon the presupposition that God is working within the individual both to will and do his own good pleasure and that he is mobilizing the fear and trembling of the person to lay hold of his own salvation, and then it will be his. For the pastoral counselor to usurp the role of " umpire," to use Job's word, is to abort the creativity that is in motion.

The author recalls vividly a young man who came to him seeking the way of religious certainty. He felt deep discrepancies between his real self and the possibilities which God was trying to reveal to him. Yet he was groping for a way that he could accept

God's purpose for his life and take the initiative to act upon his insight. A quick and easy answer from the author would have been like an umpire's decision with him, i.e., one with which he would have argued even to the point of calling the whole game off. Therefore, the author chose to live through it with him as the man sought for his own clarification. With much fear and trembling of spirit, he wrestled with his destiny under God. Most of this struggle went on apart from an interview situation, when he was all on his own. Conversations with him amounted to report meetings on the more finite issues with which he was dealing, most of which were only symbolic of deeper things about which he did not choose to talk to the author. One could only reflect as to the exact nature of these matters. Then, dramatically enough, he called on the day the second son of the author was born to express congratulations. He wanted to report too that he had come to a clear grasp of the love of God in Christ, purified of his fear of punishment.

The main issue in this man's situation was that he wanted to thank the author for exercising restraint in *not attempting to tell him everything he knew about religion, but in having the patience to provide him understanding* as he " worked out " his own salvation. A year later, the first birth date of the author's second son was marked by an unusual note from this person in another city in which he said that *in a sense* he felt himself to be exactly the same age as the young child. He felt that he had been dead and was now alive, a new creation, the workmanship of God. The main task of the counselor had been that of staying out of the way of the eternal God as he finished his new creation.

CHAPTER

9

ANXIETY AND THE FELLOWSHIP OF CONCERN

I. The Healing Power of the Cross-bearing Community

As God finishes his new creation, however, he overcomes the isolation of the individual with the first pangs of hunger for the Christian fellowship. The anxiety of the cross, fraught with holy dread as a person becomes a self before God, culminates in an inner yearning for participation in the cross-bearing fellowship of like-minded persons in the church. As the apostle Paul put it, in plighting his allegiance to the body of Christ: " Now I rejoice in my sufferings for your sake, and in my flesh I complete what is lacking in Christ's afflictions for the sake of his body, that is, the church " (Col. 1:24).

The majority of the persons whose spiritual encounters of anxiety have been recorded in these pages expressed the need to become a part of a fellowship of Christians who had had similar experiences. Strangely enough, most of them were already nominal members of the church, but now they became intensely needful of the fellowship of the church. They tended to become acutely aware of what this fellowship can actually mean to other anxious people. God mightily inspired energy within them as they became sensitive to the needs of other persons who reminded them of themselves before anything happened to change them. In this was manifested the two specific meanings of the Christian fellowship with reference to the Christian experience of anxiety: First, the loneliness of the anxious person is overcome by the power of the Holy Spirit to draw the solitary person into a spiritual community. The birth of a new self through participation in the way of the cross initiates a need for community, a search for kindred spirits. Secondly, this drive toward community transforms anxiety into social feeling, binds like-spirited persons into a consciousness of kind, issues in the establishment of the church, and converts the egocentric anxieties of men into a fellowship of caring concern for other people.

One does not sense the importance of the fellowship of a specific church until he has counseled with individuals even a few steps removed from the role of a pastor of a church. The author functions as a theological professor, as one who participates as a consultant on religious problems on the staff of a family counseling agency and of a psychiatric clinic, and as a counselor at large in a community where individuals find him personally through private contacts. He has also served as a chaplain in hospitals. In all these roles, to varying degrees of intensity the author has often " missed," with almost a type of homesickness, the definite advantages he had as a pastor of a particular church in his attempts to counsel with individuals.

The resources of casual and natural contact with individuals, the tacit power of the understood values of the Church, and the definite relationships of a specific church community necessarily must be reconstructed quite artificially in other settings such as schools, hospitals, or clinics. For instance, Maxwell Jones, a British psychiatrist, and his staff have experimented with the reordering of the whole field of relationships which affect their patient each hour of his hospital day. They have achieved observable improvements among patients who had hitherto been considered hopeless. The project followed the design of creating a therapeutic community, in which each person who had any contact at all with the patient was considered a part of the healing relationship. Even the orderlies, and particularly the nurses, were considered therapeutically significant persons. This kind of planning was the result of a growing conviction among doctors. They became convinced that the effects of a whole hour of individual psychotherapy or group psychotherapy could be negated by the blunders of an attendant on the night shift or a business administrator who did not see the relationship between the bill sent to the family and the treatment program for the patient, etc.

Maxwell Jones demonstrates that the psychiatric treatment of severe character disorders is more effective in a hospital where, in addition to the more usual methods of individual and group treatment, there is developed a therapeutic community. To achieve this end, a great deal of attention is paid to the social structure of the hospital and to the development of communication between patients, doctors, nurses, and aides.

Two remarkable results occurred in the structure of the relationship between doctors and patients: First, the doctors discovered that procedure reduced considerably the number of formal interviews necessary in psychotherapy. Instead, the doctor's relationship to his patients was carried out in numerous informal brief contacts throughout the course of the day, and interpretations, insights, etc., were developed in relation to concrete difficulties in living the individual patient was experiencing in the hospital family. Secondly, the class system between doctors and other personnel was definitely de-emphasized. The doctor divested himself of unnecessary symbols of authority such as the inevitable white coat with the stethoscope. Rather, he depended upon earning his status as a person in the life of the patient and personnel.

The morale of the hospital community was improved also. The hospital developed a certain atmosphere of fellowship and rapport. The concern of the clinical director was to take the failures of communication in the staff as bases for teaching rather than as reason for hushing up obstreperous employees, for becoming personally authoritarian, for making gory examples, etc. (Maxwell Jones, *The Therapeutic Community: A New Treatment Method in Psychiatry*. Basic Books, Inc., 1953.)

This example is drawn from a psychiatric research report for definite purposes, one of which is to show the necessity for constructing, artificially if need be, a community with healing power in all its inner relationships. And another purpose for referring to the report is to indicate that the community context and goal of even medical psychotherapy is becoming an important reality in the process of dealing with the anxieties of persons who are sick enough to be in a hospital. The hospital has tended to secularization of the healing arts of the Christian community, and in too many cases has become little more than a garage where broken machines were fixed. But the empirical discovery of the importance of the shaping existence of the spiritual community itself in healing is being realized. This approach is more than just *group* therapy, in which a few people are isolated in a highly controlled group situation for treatment. This approach involves reordering of the values and goal organization of the whole community around therapeutic achievement for the patient. It moves on the assumption that to attend to individuals' needs or small groups' needs apart from the total social fabric is to sew new cloth on an old garment.

The Christian community itself was originally intended to accomplish much of what these doctors are trying to demonstrate in their research. The contemporary failure of the Church to provide such a cleansing fellowship among men has increased to some extent at least the necessity for creating such communities apart from the Church. The contemporary successes of the Church in every known situation of mankind in developing a fellowship and community has at the same time made less necessary more such demands on the inventiveness of psychiatrists. This research project, furthermore, if applied to the context of the pastoral ministry, calls attention to the unique and intrinsic nature of the counseling done by a Christian pastor. The counseling work of a Christian pastor is essentially a function of the Christian fellowship and not of the pastor as an isolated individual. His counseling is, therefore, only one of his functions as a shepherd to whom has been entrusted the oversight of the whole flock. The pastor who seeks to become a specialist in counseling, as such, apart from the corporate life of the church, will likely move in the direction of one or more of the nonpastoral orientations to counseling and psychotherapy and away from a specifically religious kind of counseling in the context of pastoral care. The reason for this seems to lie in the essentially communal character of the counseling as done by a Christian pastor.

The pastor who restricts himself to an individualistic approach to pastoral counseling reflects a lack of awareness of the dynamic connection between pastoral administration and the processes of caring for the emotional and spiritual needs of a congregation of Christians. He is likely to neglect the needs of a great number of persons while he ministers to a selected few counselees. At the same time, he is likely to create an unrealistic expectation on the part of those few for access to his ministry in a way denied others. Furthermore, certain failures of communication can occur when a pastor deals with individuals *as if* he were not a representative of a specific congregation. (" Findings of the Commission on the Ministry," in *Conference on Counseling and Psychotherapy,* New York Academy of Sciences, 1954.) For instance, certain premarital counseling procedures with individuals can very easily create such misunderstandings if the pastor has not developed a church-wide program of family life education along with his private counseling. If he has done this, then the corporate life of the church is more likely to be edified, to feel the need for his individual counseling, and to accept and understand what he is striving to do for them. For better or for worse, the pastor is united with his spiritual community. He always carries within him the anxious tensions between the corporate resources of fellowship in his flock, on the one hand, and the aching loneliness of anxious individuals on the other hand. His counseling ministry is a means of resolving this anxiety, both as it creatively works within him and as it destructively separates his people from each other.

II. God's Reversal of Man's Anxious Loneliness

Neither pastor nor his counselee, therefore, can effectively and enduringly resolve anxiety apart from the redemptive fellowship of the Christian community. One central quality has characterized all kinds of anxiety as described in this book: *loneliness*. Economic anxiety tends to isolate men from each other; the feeling of creaturely finitude makes of mankind a " lonely crowd," to use Reisman's phrase. The grief-stricken person is likely to feel as did the Ancient Mariner: " Alone, alone, all, all alone; alone on a wide, wide sea." The sin-sick soul feels that no one could possibly understand him in his evil condition. The person suffering from the anxiety of legalism feels that he must earn his salvation singlehanded. The morally indifferent are not even aware of the need for relatedness, and how great is their unrelatedness!

As all these anxieties coalesce in the necessity of a death, burial, and resurrection, and as the individual moves into salvation " with fear and trembling," even then the anxiety of the cross and the experience of holy dread become most acute when the individual realizes that he is " alone before God." He would fain shrink back, but the act of faith calls for his staying with the struggle of the soul without an " umpire " between him and God.

But when a person moves through the depths of the experience of anxiety in the creative directions that are implicit in the intention of God for man's security, a real reversal takes place. The shrinking lonely ones turn and seek community with those who will understand from experience the real change that has taken place. The result of this movement of persons who have partaken of the sufferings of Jesus Christ is a fellowship of suffering and a fellowship of concern. The participants bear one another's burden and so fulfill the law of Christ. Those who have been comforted of God become a comfort to those who are in any affliction by means of the comfort with which they themselves have been comforted of God.

For instance, Jesus told Simon Peter that he would succumb to the stresses of temptation and forsake his Lord. But he assured him that he would be converted and that when he did he should also strengthen his brethren in their faith. This actually came to pass, inasmuch as the shaking reed who was Simon Peter before Calvary became the tower of strength at Pentecost. Likewise, the apostle Paul underwent the anxiety of the cross and the sheer terror of confrontation of God alone. The immediate aftermath of his experience was that he sought for Ananias and later turned to Barnabas, both of whom initiated him into the larger fellow-ship of the Church.

The miraculous power of the Holy Spirit indwelling in the body of Christ affects the anxieties of the participant in the Christian fellowship. The Church in all generations has experimented with communal fellowships, the aim of which has been to overcome the power of economic anxiety through the sharing of goods. This is particularly evident in the Early Church as described in the book of The Acts. The affirmation of suffering as a nor-mal part of life in the flesh, as evidence that man is man and not God, and as being common to all mankind is a consistent prac-tice of the Church at work among men. As the apostle Paul said, no temptation has overtaken man that is not also common to man. The Christian community does not, in its best moments, attempt to cure people of being human; rather, it affirms their humanity as a basis of fellowship. This is particularly true in the way a Christian community gathers about a person in the midst of grief. The indifferent, the sin-laden, and the economic exploiters receive the ministry of the Church alike in times of grief and tragedy. Except in those situations where legalistic anxiety is the order of the day in the whole body of believers, the Church par-ticipates with the sin-laden as a visible expression of the body of Christ.

Furthermore, an ethical realism is apparent in that the redemp-tive love of a community cannot take effect by overlooking the factuality of real wrong. However, once that fact has been estab-lished, the whole objective of the community is to restore such a person " in a spirit of gentleness," under the consistent aware-ness of their own possibilities of being " overtaken in a fault." The morally indifferent, furthermore, are more likely to become unusually sensitive, as did Ananias and Sapphira, when, having come to know the depth of fellowship, they willfully cut them-selves off from it. And, finally, the Christian community is always anxiously or eagerly awaiting the entrance of a person into the new being in Christ. The focus of their great anxiety is here.

III. On Being "Genuinely Anxious"

The end intention of the gospel is just this: to release man *from* the egocentric anxieties of life over economy, over death, over grief and sin, *from* the petty defenses of a legalistic way of life and *from* callous insensitivity to ethical reality. These are the kinds of anxiety the gospel aims to release men *from*. The gospel aims to release me *to* a concern for the welfare of others, to an eager preference of one another before each other, and to the adoration of the Lord Jesus Christ. Paul could talk about his "caring" spiritual concern without any sense of abashment. He could say that "apart from other things" (being beaten with rods, being stoned, being shipwrecked, being in danger in many ways, losing sleep, being hungry, being thirsty, cold and exposed) "there is the daily pressure upon me of my anxiety for all the churches." This is what one means by *spiritual concern*. When one has been set free from the bondage of fear he can really give himself without reservation to the needs of other people. In another almost chance reference, the apostle Paul gave a flesh-and-blood illustration of all that has been said here when he spoke of Timothy to the Philippian church:

"I hope in the Lord Jesus to send Timothy to you soon, so that I may be cheered by news of you. I have no one like him, who will be genuinely anxious for your welfare. They all look after their own interests, not those of Jesus Christ." (Phil. 2:19–21.)

This kind of caring is the noblest expression of the capacity of man to be anxious. Harry and Bonaro Overstreet, in their book *The Mind Alive,* re-emphasize the importance of this anxiety in care for others when they say:

"There is, in psychological truth, a certain terror that is a part of the experience of deep caring: the terror of letting one's self go, putting one's whole capacity to feel and to suffer at the disposal of something beyond the self. No one, it seems safe to assume, who has ever deeply and genuinely loved another human being or a chosen vocation or a social cause or a religious faith has ever wholly escaped this terror."

Man cannot plan to be safe by caring less. This is the way of the morally indifferent. "If the risks of caring are great, so are the rewards; for it is one of the basic facts of human life that the *ungiven* self is the *unfulfilled* self." (Harry and Bonaro Overstreet, *The Mind Alive,* p. 105. W. W. Norton & Company, Inc., 1954.) The person who has become a self before God can give himself with an abandon that has been purged of hesitation and division of spirit. He can genuinely be anxious for nothing — that is, have no need for idolatrous defenses, no need for hesitation, and no need for fretful preoccupation of the spirit. He can cast all these cares upon God, for God is his defense, his purpose, and the inhabitant of his inner being. Then man's tightened fists and fretfully wrung hands are set free for the care of " those who are in any affliction." This is the triumphant intention of the gospel, the tree of life, the leaves of which are for the healing of the nations.